CREATING A HOME
DESIGNING AND PLANNING
BATHROOMS

WARD LOCK

CONTENTS

© Ward Lock Limited 1988
Wellington House, 125 Strand, London WC2R 0BB

Based on *Creating a Home*,
First Edition © Eaglemoss Publications Limited, 1986

Reprinted 1989, 1991, 1992, 1994 (**Twice**) , 1995

ISBN 0 7063 6734 0

Printed in Spain by Cayfosa Industria Grafica

INTRODUCTION

Whether you are planning a complete bathroom refit or just want to update what you have, this is the book to help you get the best results.

Designing and Planning Bathrooms starts off with a chapter on getting the basic planning right, followed by page after page of ideas for bathrooms to suit every taste and pocket. There's the fitted bathroom, designed to provide plenty of storage space; new looks for old bathrooms; bathrooms featuring unusual decor or unconventional fittings such as round or period style baths; and super-modern ultra-streamlined bathrooms. Further chapters deal with more specialized rooms: fitness bathrooms equipped with whirlpools and saunas; shower rooms; en suite bathrooms; loos and cloakrooms.

The bathroom is just the place to indulge a yen for way-out decor which would quickly pall in other rooms. This book is rich in examples of such fun bathrooms, designed to evoke, for example, a conservatory, a ship's cabin, a marble hall, even a gothic cathedral!

However, the practical side is given equal importance. Whatever the decor, fantastic, romantic or strictly functional, the materials used must be hardwearing and stand up to water, steam and condensation. Further chapters show the best materials to use for walls and floors; how to plan creative but practical tiling schemes; and how to box in a bath. Four buyers' guides illustrate the wide range of bath and shower room fittings on the market.

Designing and Planning Bathrooms is an essential ideas book and practical guide for anyone planning to redecorate or refit a bathroom.

ORGANIZING YOUR BATHROOM

Think carefully about plumbing, heating and ventilation when planning your bathroom.

The bathroom should be one of the most inviting rooms in your home. Try to make it a combination of warmth and luxury with the practical plus points of easy-to-clean fittings and splashproof wall and floorcoverings.

Relaxing in a hot bath, or enjoying an invigorating shower are both wonderful ways to unwind after a difficult day, but a chilly, badly decorated bathroom is no place to linger. Often a coat of paint, some thick, foam-backed carpet, fluffy towels and the addition of a heated towel rail can make the difference between discomfort and welcoming warmth. If the suite is old and in poor condition or the plumbing is antique and the space badly planned, more radical improvements are needed.

FIRST STEPS
Look through manufacturers' brochures to find a style you like. Although many of the rooms shown are larger than the average family bathroom, there are plenty of good ideas on how fittings can be arranged. Some bathroom manufacturers offer a free fitting kit.

Specialists If you can, it is worth visiting some specialist bathroom shops where you will find baths, basins and fittings in many different shapes and colours. Specialists are a good source of non-standard size baths, such as continental sit-up models. You'll also see unusual finishes, such as fake marble and metallic effects. Some specialists sell showers, including the latest 'environmental enclosures', complete with soft rain effect and piped music. All specialists have a range of taps, tiles, towels, flooring and accessories, so it is possible to do all your bathroom shopping under one roof.

Colour choice When looking at brochures, remember that colour printing can be deceptive. Most sanitaryware manufacturers supply colour samples which can be matched up with wall-coverings, flooring and tiles. Take the colour sample with you when you shop and ask if you can compare colours in natural light – shop neon changes tones.

Plumbing If you are unsure how changes might affect plumbing – and whether or not restrictions would make your plans possible, ask a plumber for a survey.

Ventilation Lack of ventilation causes condensation in bathrooms. An extractor fan fitted to the window disposes of steam without bringing in cold air. If the bathroom does not have a window, it must be fitted with a ducted fan which switches on when the light is turned on.

A ducted fan wafts steam out through ducting which travels between walls to the outside air.

STARTING FROM SCRATCH
Installing a brand new bathroom is an opportunity to get everything right. A new suite, flooring, lighting, heating and decoration give you the chance to plan a room to suit both your tastes and your lifestyle. Use the checklist below to decide what you would like in your new bathroom before you make a plan and choose the fittings.

Make a plan Measure the room in metric as sanitaryware is sold in metric sizes and draw the shape of the room on to squared paper, allowing one big square per 25cm. As well as the length, width and height of the room, mark the following on the plan.
- The position of the door and the direction in which it opens.
- Size and position of windows.
- Position of the hot and cold water supplies.
- Hot water cylinder and airing cupboard.
- Radiator or heated towel rail.
- Cold water tank.
- Electrical fittings.
- Anything you want to keep.

CHOOSING FITTINGS
Re-planning your bathroom need not mean buying new fittings. If the existing suite is in good condition but badly placed, it may be worth moving it around. Alternatively, if you hate the colour, think about having the bath and fittings re-surfaced. There are several specialist companies who offer this service. The work is done on site, there is a good choice of colours and the cost is about a quarter of the price of a new bathroom suite.

If your suite needs replacement, look through bathroom manufacturers' brochures and make a shortlist of suites which appeal to your tastes. If the house is modern in style, concentrate on the new soft, clean pastels. If you live in a period home, look at Victorian style and decorated suites.

Before you make the final plan, it is worthwhile thinking about the plumbing, space around fittings and the best way to position them.

Plumbing The WC needs to be linked to the main stack (the big pipe which goes down the outside of your house). Moving this is very difficult, so try to keep the WC in the same place.

It is cost-effective to have the WC, bidet, basin and bath in a line, so that there is one straight run of water pipes. The pipes can be hidden away behind a partition (called a plumbing duct). It may be possible to position the duct across the room so it makes a low dividing

---

BATHROOM CHECKLIST
Before you buy any sort of bathroom equipment, list what is wrong with the current room, and what you would like to have.

- **Facilities** How many bathrooms, showers and WC's do you need? If the family have left home, would you be better off with en suite facilities in the master bedroom, and a separate shower and toilet?

- **Position** Is your present bathroom in the right position?

- **Hot water** Does your present system provide enough hot water?

- **Who uses the bathroom?** Do you need to make safety provisions for old people or children?

- **The fittings** Are they in good condition or do they need replacing?

- **Your budget** How much can you afford to spend?

- **Heating** Is the bathroom warm?

- **Ventilation** Does the bathroom suffer from condensation?

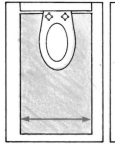
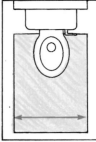

△ WC and bidet space
There should be enough space around the WC and bidet for comfortable use – about 70cm wide and 110cm space in front.

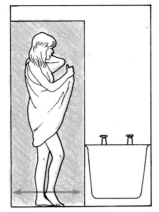

△ Beside the bath
Allow enough space (70cm minimum) beside the bath for users to climb in and out and to dry themselves.

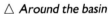
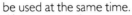

△ Around the basin
Space around the basin is important, allow 70cm wide and 110cm in front. Avoid siting deep shelves above basin.

wall. Position the bath on one side and the WC, basin and bidet on the other. If you want to hide pipes in ducting, choose a wall-hung WC, basin and bidet designed for use with ducted plumbing.

Space around fittings Sufficient floor space around fittings is important if the bathroom is to work efficiently. There should be enough space around each fitting for it to be used comfortably. At the side of the bath, allow room for the user to get in and out easily and dry himself in comfort. A standing area 70cm wide at the side of the bath is the minimum comfortable space.

Space at the front and sides of the washbasin, WC and bidet is equally important. Allow an area 70cm wide and 110cm long in front of the wash-basin. Don't position a shelf or cup-board over the basin where someone could bump their head. The WC and bidet should be set in an area about 70cm wide, with 110cm of space in front. If the WC and bidet are side-by-side, the space between them can be decreased as it is unlikely that both will

▽ Build a plumbing wall
If you site the basin, bath, bidet and WC along one wall, piping can be hidden in a duct. Shaded areas show the space needed for fittings.

be used at the same time.

If the bathroom has a separate shower cubicle, make sure the entrance is not obstructed and that there is enough space for the door to open fully. If space is limited, choose a cubicle with a sliding door. Allow about 70cm of standing space in front of the shower.

POSITIONING FITTINGS
The way fittings are positioned can help to make your bathroom practical and pleasant to use.

The bath The usual site for the bath is with one side and one or both ends hard up against a wall, but if space and plumbing permit, it is possible to achieve a more interesting layout by centring the bath along a wall, or in the middle of the floor.

If the bath is positioned with the side centred in the middle of a long wall, you can build a plumbing partition duct along the tap end and site the washbasin or WC on the other side of it. The plumbing duct wall should end at about waist height. The space above can be left open, or can be filled with shelving

or a display of plants. The advantage of doing this is that the bath is screened from the rest of the room, so more than one person can use the facilities at a time.

Another idea is to build a floor-to-ceiling tiled partition at each end of the bath so that it is enclosed in an alcove. Put the WC at one end and a shower cubicle at the other.

The washbasin If there is space, install two washbasins to ease the strain on the bathroom at peak times. Make sure that there is enough space for two people to stand at the basins. If the WC is in the bathroom, site the basin close by. Make sure, too, that there is a towel rail close to the basin and wall space for a toothbrush holder and soap dish.

WC and bidet Ideally, the WC and bidet should be separate from the bathroom, but in many homes lack of space makes this impossible. You may have very little choice on position as it depends on the location of the main soil stack, but if possible, site the WC close to a window or ventilation. The bidet should be beside the WC.

BATHROOMS FOR CHILDREN
☐ A step up to the bath makes climbing in and out easier.
☐ A shower cubicle fitted with a thermostatically controlled shower means that children can wash safely, unattended.
☐ As children have a habit of locking themselves in bathrooms and toilets, fit a lock which can be opened with a screwdriver from the outside.
☐ A plastic box on wheels makes a good home for bathtime toys.
☐ Install a locking cupboard for medicines.

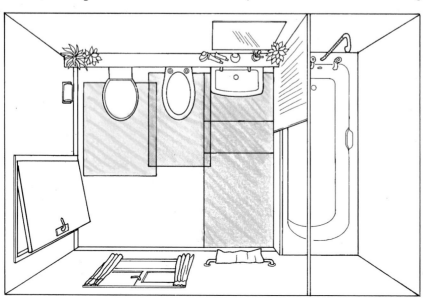

A FITTING BATHROOM

Ideas to help you turn your bathroom
from the plainly functional
to the handsomely fitted.

The bathroom is where we start and end the day, and the bleak discomfort of a cheerless room is not an inviting prospect. Until recently, bathroom design tended towards the utilitarian. Most bathrooms contained little more than the basic bath, basin and WC, with perhaps a medicine cabinet and a few shelves. At last bathrooms are receiving the attention enjoyed by other areas of the home.

In the fitted bathroom the familiar trio of bath, basin and WC can be linked with a continuous run of units, providing sleek surfaces and cupboards sealed against moisture. Systems can start with a simple vanity unit and build up to wall units, corner cupboards and open and closed shelving.

A fitted bathroom can look handsome. Accessory clutter is tidied away and a clean line given to what is often a cumbersome array of sanitaryware. You can add finishing touches to pro-vide a pleasant room to relax in – even a comfortable chair, if there's space.

If you live in an older house with a generous-sized bathroom, you could plan more ambitiously. Perhaps include a dressing area or, in these health-conscious days, have a work-out section. Think about installing laundry facilities, to deal with the used laundry where it generates. Remember, though, to comply with safety regulations – get expert advice before installing electrical appliances.

Even if you haven't space for lavish projects, modern fitments can transform a spartan washing area to a room that's a delight to use.

Storage style
A bathroom that looks fresh and inviting has been designed to make use of all available space. Open and closed storage systems allow today's pretty toiletries to be on view and conveniently to hand, while less sightly necessities are stored away.

◁ Individual style

An excellent example to prove that the modern bathroom need not be bleakly impersonal, but can offer the same degree of elegance as the rest of the home. This rich combination of traditionally-styled practical and decorative features shows how a room can reflect highly individual taste while still enjoying the benefits of modern facilities.

▽ Beech bathroom

These handsome wall-hung units would suit all but the tiniest of rooms, and the warm beech and white finish looks crisply trim and stylish. Bathroom requisites can be stored in cupboards and drawers, and open shelving gives easy access to towels and toiletries.

BATHROOM BASICS

Before you start considering choice of units, work out your plans based on the size and shape of your room: will your budget and space stretch to a full range of built-in units? Will sleek lines look out of place in an older-style or traditionally-furnished house?

A fitted bathroom needn't be brutally modern: many traditional-style units are available. Materials are the same as those used for fitted kitchens — coloured laminated plastics, various wood finishes and some luxury man-made or natural materials. Whatever the finish, rounded edges and corners are essential for safety and comfort.

The fullest range of built-in bathroom fitments extends to a wide choice of storage cupboards — full height, low level, or high level — to house everything that gathers in a bathroom. Plumbing should be housed out of view, but do be sure to provide access panels. Bath, wash basin and cistern can be encased, and work surfaces and shelving may be built in.

Off-the-peg systems would suit a bathroom of standard proportions. Though more expensive, a made-to-measure range will give flexibility and make the most of valuable space.

If your bathroom is tiny, planning of every precious centimetre is essential. Consider a basic system of a small vanity unit with storage above and below, and fit wall units or shelving as space permits.

△ *Flexibly modern*
A robust wall storage system with adjustable shelving that can be designed to suit particular needs. Here the units are shown in a sophisticated blend of ochre, grey and white.

▽ *Bathroom cheer*
A modern version of a vanity unit provides neat storage under double basins. Note how the accessories have been carefully selected to match the stylish red trim.

◁ *Panelled elegance*
A graceful dresser-style unit shows how beautiful modern bathroom furniture can be – note how carved mouldings and an arch add a fine elegance. But it's all very practical, too. There is plenty of room for storage both under and above the double basins. This sort of unit would be ideally suited to make the most of space in a small but high-ceilinged bathroom.

▽ *Practically pretty*
Another design that makes the most of all the available space, with high- and low-level storage. Even the cistern housing is incorporated into the work-surface run, with adjacent cupboard storage in an area which is not normally put to efficient use.

A PLACE FOR EVERYTHING

Once you've decided on the main units, you will have to plan efficient use of the storage space. Make a list of all the items you need to store – this will include necessities such as stocks of lavatory paper, soap and shampoo, and supplies of cleaning materials. You also need to find space for extra towels, bathrobes and perhaps linen as well as storage for used laundry. Toiletries, cosmetics and medicines all need allotted space.

If this is your only bathroom, you will need to arrange handy storage of essentials needed for peak-time family use. How often is a particular item used? For example, if you store fresh supplies of baby's nappies in the bathroom they must be readily accessible.

One of the pleasures of a fitted bathroom is that you can tuck away all the less sightly necessities like bathroom cleaners and stocks of lavatory paper. Extra towels can also be stored in closed cupboards. Medicines should be housed beyond the reach of children in a special cabinet with a lock or safety catch.

Reserve open storage – shelves and work surfaces – for items that look good, like pretty toiletries and plants that thrive in a moist atmosphere. Make sure, though, that you don't cram in too much to spoil the streamlined look of your fitted bathroom.

▷ Compact storage

With thoughtful planning, extra storage facilities can be coaxed into the smallest bathroom. Not a centimetre of space is wasted in this arrangement, where all the bathroom paraphernalia is kept conveniently within reach but neatly out of sight.

▽ Richly wooden

Natural materials can add warmth to soften the functional aspects of a modern bathroom. These sturdily attractive high- and low-level pine units provide plenty of storage, and would be ideal if you wanted to give your bathroom a robust country air.

△ **Door detail**
This view of shelving set on the inside of a wall-unit door shows how much can be kept in a very little space. Larger items such as towels are stored in the cupboard itself, with smaller toiletries shelved inside the door.

BATHROOM EXTRAS

Many modern bathroom units are provided with internal fittings to give a clever selection of concealed laundry and waste bins, wire basket storage for towels, integral mirrors and lighting, and many other extras. Most of these have borrowed inspiration from the fitted kitchen, and an enterprising DIY expert could even adapt standard kitchen fitments for bathroom use.

Corner carousels can provide valuable storage in a tight corner. Trays are designed to swivel out so you don't have to delve deep into cupboards to forage for small items – an added convenience is that makeup can be used straight from the tray. Some fitted storage ideas are very neat. Soap dishes can slide away after use to give a flush surface, and a few units even have a special built-in radio.

Though most bathroom accessories can be neatly stored, some essentials need to be left out for convenient use. Look for accessories which will complement your overall scheme, as you don't want to spoil the clean lines of a fitted bathroom with a hotchpotch of unmatched extras. Towels are generally very evident in a bathroom; choose them to match the overall scheme. Storage ideas range from wall-high heated ladders to small fitments designed to hold guest towels. Some manufacturers provide colour-matched items such as beakers, bath tidies and towel rings. For a streamlined effect, choose fitments such as soap dishes which are inset rather than projecting.

Built-in units often have integral lighting for tasks such as shaving. For applying makeup, consider Hollywood-style light bulbs set around a mirror for a touch of real glamour.

△ **Tray hold-all**
Drawer space can be fitted with trays which will keep separate little items that are so easily mislaid. Here cosmetics are stored ready for use straight from the tray.

△ **Bathroom carousel**
An idea originally developed for the fitted kitchen which works equally well in the modern bathroom. Door-mounted swivel trays give immediate access to personal toiletries.

BRIGHT IDEA

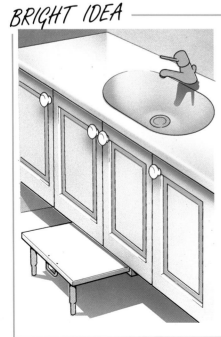

PLATFORM PERFORMANCE

Bathroom fitments are developed with adults in mind; they often leave small children with an awkward stretch to reach basin and taps.

This sturdy platform pulls out at washtime, and will help a child develop independence in the bathroom while still remaining safe. Once the child has finished, the platform slides beneath the wall-hung units to leave the way clear for other, taller, bathroom users.

Take care where you place chemicals and drugs. All medicines should of course be kept behind a childproof door that is also well beyond a child's reach. Many bathroom units now incorporate a high-level medicine cabinet.

△ **Laundry store**
The lower cupboard door of this unit swings open to allow easy disposal of used laundry. Clearing the floor space of freestanding items like laundry baskets leaves the room clutter-free.

MAKING THE MOST OF SMALL BATHROOMS

A small bathroom can be very cosy, but there's usually room for improvement.

Although catalogues from manufacturers of bathroom suites illustrate larger-than-life settings, most of us have to deal with much smaller rooms.

THE OPTIONS

If the rest of your accommodation is generous, you can make a separate shower room or toilet, freeing valuable space and reducing pressure on the bathroom itself. Or, if a room next door is large enough, you can 'borrow' some of that space and enlarge your bathroom. These solutions, however, are expensive, involving both major

plumbing works and building expenses.

More realistically, you can try to work with what you have. In terms of re-arranging the plumbing, it is relatively easy to change the position of the basin, more difficult to change the position of the bath, and hardest of all to move the toilet.

A cheaper alternative is to replace large, and perhaps outdated or ugly fittings with smaller, more compact and modern ones.

The easiest and least expensive solution is to use colour, pattern and mirrors to create an illusion of space.

High-level ideas Many small bathrooms are too high in proportion to their floor area. Transform some of this high-level space into storage: cupboards above the bath are one possibility; building a narrow shelf between the top of the door and the ceiling another. Or try continuing the ceiling colour a short distance down the walls to the line of an imaginary picture rail to improve the proportions of the room.

Neat boxing in of any messy plumbing work and clever conversion of awkward areas into concealed extra storage space will help to streamline a small room.

Cool and pretty

Crisp white panelling, fresh florals and pale blue tiles give an air of sophistication to this ordinary, rectangular bathroom. Notice how the skirting has been continued around the bath panel and into the kick recess of the vanity unit. A pretty festoon blind in a charming flowery print disguises the frosted glass window; the same fabric is used for the chair cushion. A row of flower-pattern tiles, the houseplants and prints all echo the floral theme.

△ **Stunningly simple**
Palest pink fittings with candy-striped tiles make the most of this elegant bathroom.

Clever positioning of two large sheets of mirrored glass opposite each other carry reflections to infinity and create the impression that the bath is set into an alcove. As there is no shower attachment, and the bath is set a tile's width in from the wall, shelves could be built above the end of the bath. These could be used for storing towels and other essentials.

BRIGHT IDEA

Double shower curtain If you want to use a shower curtain but can't find a ready-made one to go with your colour scheme, use a co-ordinating fabric. Punch holes in the fabric, re-inforce them, and clip on plastic rings to attach a waterproof lining.

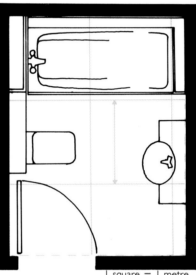

1 square = 1 metre

▷ **Off the floor**
For a really sleek effect, wall-hung fittings make for a spare, uncluttered look (floor plan above).

There wasn't enough room for a separate shower, so one has been built into the wall at the end of the bath. The strongly patterned shower curtain co-ordinates with the wallpaper border. There are glass shelves above the built-in cistern while the solid shelf next to the basin has been tiled.

SMALL AND STYLISH
Used cleverly, mirrors can appear to double the size of a room, while the clean lines of modern, wall-hung fittings, together with a sophisticated colour scheme, will help to create a sense of space.

Reflections Bathroom mirrors have far greater potential than being used just for shaving or brushing your teeth.

Mirror tiles come in all sizes, from tiny mosaic squares to huge glass panels, and range from the traditional silver to smokey grey and warm, pink-tinged tones. Tinted mirrors and small mirror tiles are kinder to less-than-perfect naked bodies than large panels of silvered mirrors.

In poorly ventilated bathrooms, condensation on mirrors can be a problem,

and glass mirror tiles feel cold to the touch. Acrylic mirrors and tiles are slightly better in this respect and are lighter in weight but are easily scratched. Make sure any mirror you buy is suitable for bathroom use, or the mirrored backing may come off.

Like ceramic tiles, mirror tiles need to be fixed to rigid, even surfaces, and large mirrors need strong, sound walls.

Fitting solutions Whether making a new bathroom or replacing existing units, remember that wall-hung basins and toilets take less floor space than conventionally supported bathroom fittings and that cleaning under them is simple. Be careful of weak internal walls; basins weigh least, but an occupied toilet is very heavy. If in doubt, consult a reputable builder or surveyor.

Although there are no scaled-down toilets, there are models with slim-line cisterns, ideal for ducting. There are also small basins, usually advertised as being suitable for bedrooms, but equally useful in tiny bathrooms. Steer clear of basins sold specifically for cloakrooms. These are too small to be useful for anything other than washing hands.

◁ *Tiling interest*
An interesting pastel scheme gives a spacious feel to a small room. Woodwork and tiling are in the same grey and are a good contrast to the pale pink walls. Tiling interest comes from the diamond pattern, which is continued around the mirror, creating a border.

▽ *Streamlined unity*
A narrow bathroom with a period feel is fitted into an area no more than 3 m by 2 m. The vanity basin unit has roomy cupboard space and the boxing in around the cistern is continued up to the ceiling to make an open-shelved dresser.

The uncluttered feel is created by building in the bath and the basin in a continuous line, matching up the line of the skirting with the bottom of the panelled fittings.

CLEVERLY CONCEALED

The smaller the bathroom, the more important it is that dull or unattractive items are kept out of sight.

If you are replacing bathroom fittings, go for the sleekest ones you can find – suites that have been designed so that the plumbing can be concealed or ducted. Alternatively, you can combine clean lines with hidden storage space by boxing in your fittings.

If the toilet and basin range along one wall, and the supply and waste pipes are laid in a single line, the whole lot, including a slimline cistern, can be hidden behind a purpose-built false wall, finished to match the scheme of the bathroom. The top of the wall can be used as a narrow shelf for accessories or ornaments. (Make sure you can open a panel to gain access to the pipes and cistern.)

Storage If the cistern is on a long wall, boxing it in could include shelving on either side or above.

Boxing in the basin is a smaller scale project, and there are ready-made vanity units available from manufacturers. If the front is fitted with a door, you will have the perfect hideaway for shampoo bottles, cleaning materials and spare toiletries.

TIGHT ON SPACE

If you have a really small bathroom, perhaps where you have 'borrowed' space to make it en suite with an adjoining bedroom, you may not have the room to fit in a conventional bath.

The obvious answer is a shower but, for those who prefer a bath, a sit-down model provides an up-to-the-neck soak. In the room on the right this arrangement enables you to have bath, toilet and basin without overcrowding.

To avoid a small room becoming claustrophobic, keep your colour schemes simple – go for clean lines, either with light, neutral backgrounds to help create a sense of space, or choose a single clear colour for a brighter effect. This is not the place for unnecessary clutter, so keep it all out of sight; built-in storage is a definite bonus in this situation.

A real plus in a small bathroom is that you can splash out on a few more expensive materials than usual – tiles, fabrics and flooring – without breaking the bank.

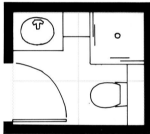

1 square = 1 metre

△ Deep water
Where there is no space for a conventional bath, consider a sit-down model. Using pale wall and floor tiles gives a quiet, restful mood to this very small room. The neutral scheme also helps blur the boundaries between the floor, walls and sides of the bath, lending a sense of space.

◁ Mellow yellow
The alternative solution is a shower cubicle to replace the bath (floor plan above). This time the colour scheme is simple but stunning – all white fittings and tiles in the shower contrasted with bright yellow vinyl wallpaper, rubber flooring and accessories. A corner opening shower door is the best choice for this tight space.

◁ **Country look**
This bathroom in an older house has been given a country feel by taking easily cleaned gloss-painted tongued-and-grooved boarding up to windowsill level. This is higher than a normal dado but is very practical in a bathroom. The bath has been set 15cm in from the window wall, thus creating a useful shelf.

The 'dead area' above the toilet is taken up with a roomy kitchen cabinet, painted to match the boarding with a front panel covered in the same paper as the walls.

A wide and wonderful wallpaper border defines the perimeters of the room and outlines the fairly small window.

△ **Hidden storage**
Sliding mirrored cupboards not only double the apparent size of this compact room, but give plenty of storage space. This very neat solution does, however, have a snag; the mirrors really must be kept immaculate or the whole effect is spoilt. There is a special liquid available which can be applied to mirrors to help minimize misting in a steamy bathroom.

◁ **Bright primaries**
There is no reason why you shouldn't use colour boldly in a bathroom. Here, areas of primary red and blue are teamed with a greater amount of white – fittings, paintwork and walls – and the wallpaper above the dado picks up the primary colours in a small stylized design.

NEW LOOKS FOR OLD BATHROOMS

If you are not happy with the way your bathroom looks, think about how you can make it more stylish.

If your existing bathroom is looking tired and outdated, it is not difficult to improve on what you have. Even if you find it is too small for your family's needs there are ways round the problem.

Better use of space Rearranging the fittings can make a surprising difference to the usable area, particularly if you rehang a door that opens into the centre of the room so that it opens back against a wall. If the existing layout is really not making the best use of the available space, it is obviously well worth replacing the fittings at the same time as repositioning them. Experiment with squared paper and cut-outs of your bath, basin and so on to find the best arrangement.

If a new layout is not viable, one answer could be to knock a bathroom and next-door toilet into one. This larger space may allow you to include two wash basins and/or a shower cubicle to help with the morning rush.

Other possibilities are to take in an adjacent passageway to make a bigger bathroom or to take some space from a next-door bedroom by moving the partition wall.

An extra bathroom If you have one large bedroom, it might be a better plan to sacrifice part of it to make a small en suite bath or shower room to relieve pressure on the main bathroom.

New look

A dilapidated bathroom (right) can be revived simply by redecorating. Bringing the ceiling colour a little way down the walls and covering the top of the window with a festoon blind are both ways of visually lowering the ceiling.

A great transformation has taken place in a similar room (below). Large mirrors add a much needed illusion of space and actually do multiply the level of light in the room. The windowsill has been built up by two tile widths, the bath is placed under the window and a new vanity unit updates the old basin. Crisp white with blue tiles and blind make the room light and airy.

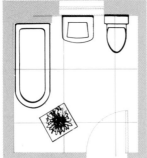

△ **Austere original**
This rather grim bathroom in
an Edwardian house is in
desperate need of
redecoration. Although the
original roll-top bath has
been painted and has lost
its claw feet, and the bath
taps are beyond repair, most
of the period fittings are
in good condition and suit
their setting far better
than modern ones.

scale: 1 square = 1 metre

NEW VERSUS OLD

Before you start ripping out all your old bathroom fittings
and replacing them with brand new ones, look at them
carefully. If they are in good condition you might only need to
change the decoration – new tiling, paint and wallcovering and
possibly some new taps can be enough to effect a complete
transformation.

You may find that your old bath is of better quality than
most modern ones around today. Cast iron baths, for
instance, were once commonplace but are now fairly difficult
to find, as well as being expensive. If the only thing wrong with
the bath is worn enamel or calcium deposits, it is possible to
have it re-enamelled.

When renovating older properties, many people go to
great lengths to track down period bathroom taps and fittings
which have been thrown out by 'improvers'. If you live in an
old house, or would like to create a traditional bathroom,
there are a growing number of architectural salvage companies who deal in all sorts of period fixtures and fittings.
There are also many manufacturers of reproduction sanitaryware, taps and accessories.

◁ **Authentic mood**
Here the atmosphere of the period has
been recreated and the room given a
homey cosiness. The bath has been
renovated and the floor and woodwork
are coated with glossy mahogany
varnish. Plain dark green tiles were
chosen for the area below the dado,
with an edging of hand-decorated
green/brown/white ones.
　　The Edwardian love of green plants is
acknowledged by a leafy wallcovering
and a hanging potted fern.

▽ **Modern setting**
The same room adapts well to a more
modern treatment. The outside of the
bath is painted grey with a black and
yellow stencilled border to match the
painted dado. The same three colours
are used for the vinyl tiled floor.

BATHROOM FACELIFTS

The largest part of revamping an existing bathroom is the expense of plumbing and new fittings. If you inherit a bathroom where everything works perfectly but just doesn't suit your taste, there are ways of changing the whole mood of the room without having to start from scratch.

Using colour and pattern Look at the colours of the fittings and tiles or anything else you can't afford to change, and make that your starting point. A wallpaper that picks up one or more of these colours in a bold pattern can look stunning, especially if it is emphasized by curtains and accessories that match or co-ordinate.

Even if it's very small, there's no reason why the bathroom shouldn't have style. Rich, full-length curtains or a decorative austrian blind brighten up the dullest windows.

A pastel-coloured, mini-print wall-covering, especially if it is used on the ceiling as well as the walls, can visually extend a small or dark bathroom. If light colours are used for the flooring and curtains, too, the effect is increased.

The bathroom no longer has to be a plain, functional and rather cold place that you spend as little time in as possible. As long as it is heated adequately, it may only take the addition of a fitted carpet or thick rugs for it to be really warm and cosy, and a comfortable chair or elegant window seat can make it a truly inviting room.

△ Pretty in pink

The plain white tiles and fittings of this small bathroom made it feel a rather cold and bleak place.

The new owners left the bath and very useful vanity basin unit as they were. They papered the walls with a warm pink mini-print vinyl covering and hung matching shower curtain and blind. Keeping the soap and towels pink and adding the potted cyclamen provide the finishing touches.

◁ Luxurious looks

Instead of choosing pale or neutral colours to go with the strong blue fittings and mustard tiles, a daring approach was adopted. Bold floral wallpaper in a close-related yellow with blue among other accents brings the room alive. Matching fabric is used for the elegant upholstered seat in front of the window and for the full-length curtains caught back with a silk tie at below-sill level. The large print above the bath has the same colours used in different proportions to pull the whole look together.

△ *Trellis effect*
The rather predictable pink fittings in this small modern bathroom have been transformed by adventurous pink and green trellis wallpaper used not only on the walls and ceiling but on the side of the bath (protected by a clear panel).

BRIGHT IDEA

WAYS WITH WINDOWS
A boring frosted glass window or one that looks out on a dull view can be made more interesting.
☐ A sheet of caning cut to fit inside the window frame can be held in place against the glass with quarter-round beading.

☐ Glass shelves fitted across a window look very attractive with a collection of small glass bottles or ornaments and potted plants standing on them.

Supported by slim brackets at either end, the shelves still allow some light through.

☐ As an alternative to net curtains or blinds, you can cover clear glass with self-adhesive vinyl made to look like stained glass for a period look.

It is easy to apply and easy to keep clean. Fairly small panes look best with this treatment.

QUICK CHANGE

The least expensive way to change the look of a bathroom is to add new accessories such as a matching mirror, tooth mug holder and soap dish. Pale or neutral coloured fittings set against plain walls and floors are the most versatile bases from which to work.

In a white or cream room you can add a flowery festoon blind, pick out two or three of the colours for towels and add a wooden toilet seat and towel rail for a country look. Alternatively, you could choose a roller blind with a strongly coloured geometric design and take one colour from this to use as an accent.

Stylish setting

A classic white suite, a black and white tiled floor and chrome fittings are set against creamy walls (left). The look is spacious and smart but the mood is rather bleak.

The introduction of just one strong colour – a bluey-green – immediately makes this a more interesting scheme (below). The chrome trolley, mirrors and the pictures well-placed over the basins and bath further improve it. A couple of dramatic plants are the perfect finishing touch.

UNUSUAL BATHROOMS

A special bathroom can be created through the decoration or the shape and style of the bath itself.

A large bathroom, or one which is an odd shape, offers almost unlimited scope for creating an unusual atmosphere. But even a small, rectangular bathroom can, with a little ingenuity, be turned into something out of the ordinary. And an unexciting bathroom suite can be totally transformed if it is imaginatively combined with out-of-the-ordinary patterns and materials.

The fittings, too, can transform a bathroom. The traditional materials for baths – cast iron and steel – are rigid, stable and durable as well as cold to the touch and extremely heavy. Modern materials are not only lighter in weight and warmer to the touch, they are also easily moulded – making it possible to incorporate backrests, seats and even inset soap trays. Hence the modern generation of baths, many of which are a far cry from standard traditional rectangular shapes.

Corner baths, round baths, and sit-in baths all look, and feel, distinctive. Whirlpool baths have the added bonus of providing gentle underwater massage in addition to a warm soak. Baths which reproduce the elegance of the Victorian and Edwardian eras are increasingly widely available.

Finally, of course, you may want to choose a non-standard bath for practical as well as decorative reasons – to fit into a small space or make use of an odd angle, perhaps.

Period elegance
Attention to detail is the hallmark of this traditionally-styled bathroom. While they are in keeping with the overall style, the accessories also incorporate modern conveniences such as a shower attachment and a heated towel rail.

◁ **Richly panelled**
Wood panelling on the bath, vanity unit and drawers produces a warm, unfussy atmosphere. The tongued-and-grooved panelling on the walls has been laid diagonally, with alternating light and dark panels, to create added interest in what could otherwise become a rather dark expanse of wood.

▷ **Conservatory style**
For an exotic look, you can't beat a round bath! Where there isn't space for a round bath in the centre of the room, the bath can be positioned along a wall using angled panels. The floorcovering has been extended to cover the bath surround, for an uninterrupted look.

▽ **Flowery co-ordination**
Many period-style baths are supplied unfinished on the outside. This means that you can simply paint the bath with gloss or eggshell paint in the colour of your choice – or you can try more adventurous techniques such as rag rolling, dragging or stencilling. These charming sprays of flowers were hand-painted to match the wallpaper.

STYLISH BATHS

Not all baths are rectangular – many interesting shapes and sizes are available as part of manufacturers' standard ranges. So finding a bath which meets your special requirements should pose no problems.

The simplest variations differ little from the common rectangular shape. Shorter-than-usual baths are available to fit into smaller-than-usual rooms – and there are also extra-long baths for tall people. Contoured baths which are waisted in the middle, tracing the outline of the human body, are both comfortable and economical on water.

Corner baths not only look different, they can also be extremely practical. Many have a built-in shelf or ledge – ideal for sitting children on or resting your novel or magazine safely out of the wet. Since the sides of the smallest corner bath are 1200mm in length (considerably shorter than the conventional 1600/1700mm), they are particularly suited to small en suite or irregularly-shaped bathrooms.

Round baths provide a taste of 'hollywood-style' bathing, but also re-quire a 'hollywood-sized' bathroom to create the desired effect!

Whirlpool baths are also known as spa baths or Jacuzzis. Nozzles in the sides of the bath pump out pressurized streams of water to massage as well as cleanse.

Sit-in baths are square and squat in shape, ideal where space really is in short supply.

Period baths incorporate the elegant details of Victorian and Edwardian designs – fluted or scalloped edges, decorative patterns, brass taps and accessories. They also take advantage of up-to-date materials and technology. Modern conveniences such as bidets as well as baths and basins are available.

Some period baths are freestanding with ball and claw legs; others are elegantly enclosed in wooden panelling. Basins are frequently inset into wooden washstands or vanity units. WCs usually have wooden seats.

A touch of flamboyance To locate a really special bath, consult one of the growing number of bathroom special-ists, where you might find a striking heart-shaped or hexagonal bath – or even a bath for two!

BRIGHT IDEA

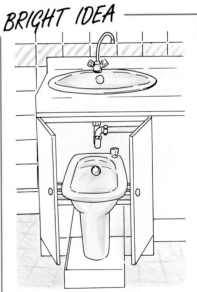

A roll-out bidet is ideal for a small bathroom. The bidet sits on a platform mounted on iron castors, making it easy to roll out from beneath the basin. Flexible pipes link the bidet to the basin, and the flow of water is controlled by a diverter similar to that found on shower attachments above baths.

A TOUCH OF LUXURY

You may eventually tire of a fancy bathroom suite which at first seems stunning, so it's often best to stick to something fairly simple, and go to town on the decoration instead. Repainting a wall is cheaper than buying a new bath!

Since the bathroom is a private place, and you don't actually live in the room, colours, patterns and styles which you couldn't tolerate elsewhere in the home can be used to good effect. (Don't, though, get too carried away: check that the materials you want to use can resist heat, damp and steam.) Lighting can reinforce the atmosphere – bright lights for a high-tech effect or glowing lighting for something more intimate.

Also consider the positioning of the suite – a bath at right angles to the wall can make an interesting focal point. Similarly, an ordinary bath can be transformed if the surround is fully tiled, panelled, or carpeted. A sunken bath invokes a feeling of luxury – and if you can't sink the bath into the floor, build up the floor instead.

△ *A hint of colour*
Simplicity of line and a plain colour scheme work together to make the most of the confined space in this bathroom. The room is fully tiled so that the walls, floor, bath surround, vanity unit and even the plumbing form a single visual entity.

The almost clinical feel is relieved by fine stripes in the tiles, while accessories in muted colours enhance the streamlined, uncluttered look.

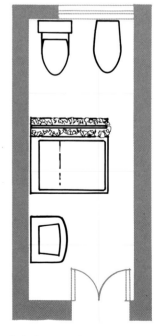

△ *Making space*
In order to squeeze all the fittings into a small bathroom, it is often necessary to make compromises. To free space in this long, narrow bathroom for a bidet as well as a bath, WC and washbasin, the original standard-sized bath was replaced by a much smaller sit-in bath. A half-height wall was then constructed in order to screen off the bath from the WC and bidet.

Scale: I square = I metre square

▷ **A second bathroom**
If you would like to add an extra bathroom to your home but haven't enough space for a standard bath a small bath may answer your problem. Extra-short baths are available which can be under 100cm long. They are ideal for children and perfectly adequate for occasional use by visitors.

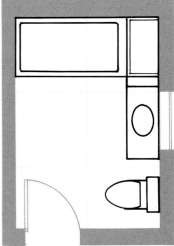

Scale: 1 square = 1 metre square

◁ **Adding a shower**
Since a small bath makes a good base for a shower, a brass shower head has been installed. The shower curtain, hung from a brass shower rail to match the taps, keeps the rest of the room free from splashes.

Patterned tiles look attractive in a small room so long as they are part of a complete colour scheme – here they co-ordinate with the blue and white of the side panels of the bath.

▷ Fantasy in wood and brass

The bathroom is a good place to indulge decorative whims and fancies that might prove tiring elsewhere in the home.

The almost cathedral-like atmosphere in this bathroom has been built up around an ordinary white bath panelled in dark wood to match the elaborately carved wood and glass panels which partially surround it.

Suitable unusual fittings can often be found at architectural salvage yards. A similar (if slightly less dramatic) effect could be created without the carving by replacing the antique panels with large mirrors and panes of glass enclosed in elaborate frames.

◁ Extravaganza in pink and blue

A little imagination and a lot of courage can create a dream-like environment in an ordinary, rectangular bathroom with standard fittings.

The walls have been divided into three zones. The lowest section visually links the bath and basin. The middle blue section is splattered with pink and two shades of blue, linking the blue of the floor and the ceiling. Finally, the uppermost section (above a narrow glass shelf) is painted dusky pink to match both the beading around the bath and the pattern in the blue section of the wall. The gleaming bathroom suite adds a crisp note and reflects the surrounding colours.

An arched, recessed mirror turns the basin into a striking feature, and carefully-chosen accessories add the finishing touches to this very individual bathroom.

BATHROOM SURFACES

Surfaces need to be practical as well as attractive to survive the extreme conditions in a bathroom.

Extremes of temperature, steam and moisture all take their toll on a bathroom surprisingly quickly. Surfaces need to be tough, waterproof and easy to maintain if they are to survive bathroom conditions and look good.

The most common materials are paint, wallpaper, tiles, or a combination. The colder, harder and shinier the surface, the more it will suffer from condensation. Mirrors and windows are the first to mist up and steam will turn quickly to water against a tiled wall.

CONDENSATION

Unless a bathroom is kept warm and well-ventilated, moisture in the air from a steaming hot bath or shower condenses, streaming down the walls and misting up mirrors and windows. In a small bathroom or in one without a window, the problems are multiplied.

The two basic ways to deal with condensation are to install an extractor fan for ventilation and to keep the bathroom at a constant heat.

Ventilation To stop the bathroom misting up, it is essential to allow the moisture-laden air to escape. Fans that rely on convection should be positioned high on the outside wall, removing the warm, wet air as it rises. Motorized extractors are more efficient, sucking the moist air out.

Warmth There are several kinds of instant heater if you don't have central heating or want to boost the temperature during the winter; wall-fixed fan heaters or radiant fires warm up a room quickly and, although inadequate on its own, a heated towel rail gives some background heat.

White practicality

Wall-to-ceiling tiling is, perhaps, the ultimate answer to the need for a waterproof and washable environment. Here, not only the walls but also the bath and basin surrounds are covered in classic white tiles. Red detail and a scarlet vinyl floor break up the otherwise stark and shining whiteness.

WALLCOVERINGS

Wallpapers, vinyl and foil wallcoverings are perfectly suitable for bathrooms, and patterns are great disguisers of uneven surfaces.

Wallpaper requires a sound smooth surface that has been well prepared and sized before it is hung. For best results, always use a fungicidal adhesive. Wallpaper can absorb a small amount of moisture but in really damp conditions it may start to peel and curl at the edges and joins, although sealants are available which provide a clear protective coat. Always test a sealant on a small area first to check that your paper is colour-fast.

Although washable wallpaper cannot withstand repeated scrubbing, it can be washed down fairly vigorously.

Vinyl is more expensive than ordinary wallpaper, but more robust due to the layer of vinyl fused on to a stout paper backing. It is also tough and moisture-resistant.

Plain textured vinyls can be used to simulate those fabric coverings which would be unsuitable in a bathroom — silk, hessian, grass-cloth, for example. Others convincingly mimic the appearance of ceramic tiles at less cost; they are also warmer to the touch than ceramic.

Foil wallcoverings are steam-resistant and highly light-reflective, making them excellent for dark rooms that don't get much sunlight.

▷ *Opulent looks*
An attic bathroom can appear poky but this one looks good and is also practical.

Most of the available surfaces, including the airing cupboard doors, are covered in a mini-print paper, offset by patterned tiles which protect the splashback areas around the bath and between the basin and mirror. Bold floral curtains either side of the bath give extra height to the sloping ceiling.

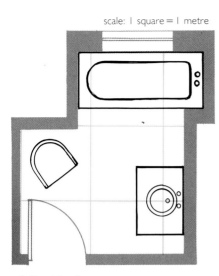

◁ *Seaside theme*
The walls in this pale bathroom are
covered in a practical vinyl wallpaper,
resilient enough to withstand splashes
and drips. The woodwork is painted in
white gloss and the bath panel is
covered in matching wallpaper
protected by a coat of clear
polyurethane.

▷ *Pastel alternative*
A different vinyl wallcovering is the basis
for this ice-cream coloured scheme.
Pale pink tiles in the alcove around the
shower, under the window and behind
the basin make a practical splashback.
Beaded wooden panels, painted pink,
blue and green, are now fitted along the
bath and under the basin.

PAINT

The cheapest and easiest way to decorate bathroom walls is to paint them with an oil-based paint, either eggshell or silk finish. Gloss is not advisable on walls as it tends to highlight the effects of condensation, can cause glare, and shows up imperfections on uneven wall surfaces. Emulsion is easy to apply and is a good disguiser of surface defects but is not so easy to wash.

Traditional paint effects such as sponging, rag-rolling and marbling work well in bathrooms. The durable coloured glazes used in many of these techniques make them particularly suitable for steamy environments.

TILING

Glazed ceramic wall tiles are the most practical work surface of all and can be used from floor to ceiling, up to dado rail height, or just around splash areas. Tiling a whole room can be costly, but it is a once-only investment that is usually worthwhile in terms of durability.

The variety of patterns, sizes, colours and textures available has largely dispelled the cold and clinical image of tiles, and there are prices to suit most pockets. Tiling a bathroom is a straightforward job and, if you are a DIY enthusiast, one that you can do yourself.

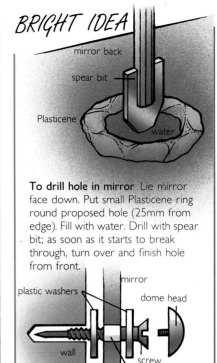

BRIGHT IDEA

mirror back

spear bit

Plasticene

water

To drill hole in mirror Lie mirror face down. Put small Plasticene ring round proposed hole (25mm from edge). Fill with water. Drill with spear bit; as soon as it starts to break through, turn over and finish hole from front.

plastic washers

mirror

dome head

wall

screw

plastic sleeve

Fix mirror Use screws with dome covers. Fit plastic washers either side of mirror. Protect hole with plastic sleeve. Don't overtighten screws in case mirror cracks.

△ *Totally tiled*
The white tiled floor and walls and large mirror by the bath are a good choice in this small, high-ceilinged bathroom. The hard-edged effect is softened with plants, shells and fluffy towels.

Plain or patterned tiles can be used to equally good effect in a modern or, as here, a more old-fashioned bathroom.

◁ *Special effects*
Practical tiling to dado height is combined with the sophisticated marbled paint technique on the walls above. This effect is achieved by blending pastel green, pale cream and grey paint with a fine paintbrush and a sponge. Use a glaze or vinyl matt paint if you use special paint effects in a bathroom and protect your hard work from steam with a coat of clear matt varnish.

▷ *Diamond design*
A tiled surface on a vanity unit is a useful and practical place to put bottles of shampoo and dishes of soap. Extending the diagonals up the splashback makes these plain white tiles look more distinctive. The two small mirrors continue the diamond pattern and are emphasized by an edging of wooden beading to match the louvred cupboard doors and window frame.

▷ **Classic simplicity**
Veneered wood has been
stained and varnished for the
bath panel and for the
surround of the unusual inset
brass basin. A matching dark
wooden, slatted blind over
the window directly above
the bath is easy to wipe clean
and preserves privacy while
allowing light into this small
room. Splash-resistant,
rag roll-effect vinyl wallpaper
gives an interesting texture
to the walls.

◁ **Half panelled**
Tongued-and-grooved
panelling in a bathroom feels
warm, is practical and
provides a good level of
insulation. In this traditional-
looking bathroom, panelling
up to the dado rail conceals
the poorly plastered walls.
To protect it from steam and
water, the wood has been
painted in a creamy coloured
vinyl matt paint.

   Above the rail, the uneven
walls are disguised by
marbled wallpaper in cream,
pale green and peach.

BATHROOM FLOORS

Aesthetics combine with the practical to produce a multitude of flooring materials suitable for bathrooms.

For most people, choosing a bathroom floor is first and foremost a practical concern. It will get splashed, it must not be slippery when wet, and it must be easy to keep clean. These factors are still more important when it comes to family bathrooms, or those used by young children or old people – bathroom fittings are, by nature, solid and angular, and will not make for a soft landing should you slip. Bathroom floors are defined as being hard or soft, and a multitude of designs and surface finishes fall into these two categories. So, though for most people practical and safety considerations play an important role, don't neglect the aesthetic qualities of the various flooring materials.

Hard floors include marble tiles and slabs, terracotta and ceramic tiles. Un-glazed tiles and those with a non-slip finish or textured surface are especially suitable. Floorboards can be polished, varnished, or painted, though the last two finishes are easier to maintain as polished floorboards will mark when they are splashed with water, leaving white stains.

Cork, rubber, linoleum, and vinyl (cushioned vinyl is a soft flooring), are all versatile, hardwearing and easy to maintain, provided you choose a reputable make. If you choose rubber, look at the textured finishes carefully: such a floor is obviously a sensible choice, but some rubber stud floorings are very bumpy, and cleaning around the studs is laborious. Vinyl flooring comes in tile and sheet form, and in many designs, patterns and colours. The most slip-resistant vinyl floors are contract quality, made for use in hospitals and other public buildings, where safety standards are very strictly regulated.

Soft finishes include cushioned vinyl and carpets. Though ordinary carpeting can be used, it is advisable to specify a bathroom quality carpet as this has a rubberized backing and cotton or synthetic pile so it will not rot or get smelly when it gets wet. Remember, as well as a damp atmosphere and splashed water, bathroom carpets are sometimes subjected to a liberal dusting of talcum powder as well! In a small bathroom, therefore, it may be sensible to get a pastel coloured or patterned carpet that is machine washable for easy care and maintenance.

New angles
Black sanitaryware is an unusual choice, but in this bathroom it looks terrific. The brilliant white ceramic tiles are a perfect foil to the WC and bidet. Black tiles have been used to form a pattern on the bath panel.

Equally unusual is the attractive and hardwearing bathroom floor, created by laying rectangular marble tiles on the diagonal. This introduces interest without detracting from the unfussy, uncluttered lines of the black and white scheme.

◁ **Practical wit**
This simple and effective floor uses squares of plywood which have been 'colour washed' with diluted grey paint. Interest has been added by laying the plywood tiles with the grain running alternately at right angles. A witty touch are the footprints, painted on to the colour-washed plywood tiles before they were sealed with three coats of varnish.

The tongued-and-grooved boards used to panel the bath have been given a similar treatment to the floorboards. Instead of using diluted paint (roughly 1 part paint:10 parts water), consider using one of a range of new-look translucent paints, which are halfway between a varnish and a paint.

◁ **Carpet for comfort**
This large and airy bathroom, with simple white sanitaryware, is far from dull. The mustard yellow colour of the towels and accessories is used to paint angular designs on the wall. The use of a white carpet softens the effect, as its textured and non-reflective qualitites generate a feeling of warmth. Pleasant to walk on in bare feet, carpets will last longer if you use bath mats, especially next to showers.

▷ **Period piece**
An elegant and old-fashioned cast iron bath with ornate legs dominates this bathroom. A hand-painted stencilled design runs around the bath, and the same gentle greens are used in the ceramic tiles, the armchair and the painted designs on the floor.

    The floor is made up of plywood tiles, prepared and painted white before being stencilled in green and pink. Although stencilled floors take a certain amount of time and planning, you are guaranteed a highly individual result. Several coats of a high-gloss varnish were applied to seal the floor. Green and white wall tiles have been fixed diagonally, and have been finished with stylish leafy tiles and curved ceramic coving tiles.

▷ Japanese style
Narrow floorboards have been painted with black gloss paint and then varnished to create a hardwearing and durable floor. The same approach is apparent throughout the bathroom, from the screens which frame the sunken bath to the kimono displayed opposite the bath. The streamlined built-in storage units incorporate the basin and ensure that the bathroom is kept relatively clear of clutter.

▽ Stylish cork
Natural cork tiles, provided they are the correct quality, create a very pleasant effect. They are warm, springy underfoot, and durable when properly sealed. In this bathroom, the cork tiles have corners that match the dark maroon of the sanitaryware, forming neat diamond patterns on the floor. The same colour is picked out on the mouldings of the panelled cupboards, to link all the fittings together. The fern suspended over the bath is a wise choice as it is a plant which flourishes in a warm and steamy atmosphere.

AROUND THE HANDBASIN

Consider the area around the handbasin carefully when choosing bathroom fittings, storage and accessories.

The handbasin and its surroundings are the functional heart of the bathroom. It's here that most activities — from making up to shaving — take place, so it follows that most equipment and accessories are necessarily grouped around the basin. Storage, lighting, a mirror and so on must all be provided.

As always, it is best to plan ahead: don't be tempted into buying an eye-catching item on impulse. Bathroom furniture and accessories come in a vast array of styles, colours and materials; shop around in order to assemble a personal selection.

Do you want a fitted look, with streamlined, built-in cupboards offering a maximum amount of hidden storage? Or would you prefer to keep more of your toiletries on display, and within easy reach when needed? Would traditional or modern fittings be most in keeping with the style of your bathroom? Should the colours be plain white, dark hardwood — or perhaps bright primaries?

Bathroom furniture and accessories can be made from wood, laminate, or plastic; accessories are also available in chrome, china and porcelain.

Honey-coloured pine or dark hard-wood is warm to the touch; sealed with a polyurethane varnish, wood can resist the damage inflicted by heat and steam.

Laminates and plastic are both ideal for bathroom use since they are hard-wearing, easy to clean and come in bright colours and delicate shades.

Chrome accessories, which were particularly popular in the 1920s and 1930s, complement the chrome taps that are still commonly found in today's bathrooms. And brass creates a luxurious effect. For a prettier, less masculine look, choose china or porcelain which is often decorated with delicate flowers or birds. Beware, though — china is easy to break or chip.

Fitted elegance
The sleek lines of fitted bathroom units combine open shelving and closed cupboards. Light fittings above the basin provide excellent task lighting — and elegant wooden rails on either side keep towels close to hand.

△ **Double basin**
A white suite is elegantly partnered by dark wood panelling; louvred doors hide storage below the double basin.

◁ **Pine units**
A separate vanity unit and a cabinet with its own mirror and light fitting create a semi-fitted look. The accessories are also made of pine to match the furniture.

THE FITTED LOOK

As well as making the best possible use of the usually limited space available in many modern bathrooms, fitted furniture also creates clean, simple lines and banishes a great deal of clutter. A bathroom can incorporate as many built-in cupboards as a fitted kitchen – a more modest fitted bathroom need include no more than a single wall-mounted or floorstanding unit.

The most basic fitted furniture is a cupboard below the basin to utilize the normally wasted space beneath. Vanity units which fit around the basin, and wall-hung bathroom cabinets are available in many different sizes and styles. Look for versions which include extras such as a mirror-door, electric shaver socket and light fitting.

BRIGHT IDEA

CONCERTINA MIRROR

Where possible, a mirror should be hung above a basin, ideally so that you can see yourself from the back as well as the front. One way to achieve this is to fix a concertina mirror next to another mirror so that it can be pulled out to reflect the view from behind.

A concertina mirror is also useful when a basin must be positioned below a window and there is no space to hang a mirror on the wall above.

A word of caution: always check that the magnifying side of the concertina mirror faces away from fabrics to prevent them scorching or even catching fire in strong sunlight.

△ **Adjustable shelving**
Open shelving provides cheap and attractive storage. The blue uprights neatly frame the mirror, and the spacing between the brackets is adjustable.

▷ **1930s feeling**
Teamed with stark black and white tiles and fittings, chrome bathroom fittings create an atmosphere which is both stylish and streamlined.

STORAGE ON DISPLAY

Although a bathroom with plenty of built-in storage is easy to keep neat and tidy, it has the disadvantage of hiding all the personal bits and pieces that produce a lived-in feel. Today's toiletries are often so beautifully packaged that it is a pity to hide them away behind cupboard doors.

Open shelves allow cosmetics to be kept on hand. Although glass shelves look smart, they require frequent cleaning to remove grubby marks. Wood and laminate are both good alternatives. Stacking vegetable trays and plastic-coated racks can be adapted for use in the bathroom; a trolley on wheels can be pushed aside when not in use.

Cleaning materials and medicines are best kept out of sight; in a household which includes small children, they should be locked away behind a child-proof catch. Consider installing a cupboard or bathroom cabinet.

FINISHING TOUCHES

Whatever style you are aiming for in a bathroom, the finishing touches can make or mar the effect. To avoid a bitty feel, look for co-ordinated accessories to complement the fittings and decor.

Combined with a white suite, carefully chosen accessories will themselves help to create the desired look. For example, a wooden clothes horse, a marble-topped washstand, brass taps, and a mahogany toilet seat can set the scene for a Victorian-style bathroom.

Rather than replace a perfectly serviceable suite because you don't like its colour or style, use accessories to transform the look of the room. If, for example, you have inherited an avocado-coloured suite, your first reaction may be to choose pale green towels and delicate china fittings. Instead, try crisp navy and white accessories and use coral as an accent colour.

Similarly, a primrose bathroom can be brought up to date with a two-tone grey scheme: perhaps pale and charcoal grey towels with a striped blind and chrome toothmug and toilet-roll holder.

△ ▷ *Colour co-ordination*

To make it easier to achieve complete co-ordination in your bathroom, pick and choose items from a range of matching bathroom accessories. Most ranges include the basics such as soap dishes, toilet-roll holders, towel rails, shelves, toothbrush holders, waste bins and laundry baskets. Others also offer extras such as door and cabinet handles, taps and shower attachments – even toilet seats.

In the bathroom pictured on the right, sunny yellow accessories add life to a pale grey suite and white cabinets. Cherry red accessories make the almost identical bathroom shown above even livelier. In both cases, the wallcovering, coloured grouting and matching roller blinds and towels complete the effect.

If you shop around, you should be able to find accessories in many colours – from the bright primaries shown in these two rooms to the natural wood, brass, and subtle pastels such as dusty pink and sage green illustrated below.

EN SUITE BATHROOMS

Add a touch of luxury and relieve pressure on family facilities with your own en suite bathroom.

The pressures on a family bathroom, particularly at peak times like the morning rush hour, can be considerable. In such circumstances, it would be a rare family that wouldn't welcome the addition of an extra bathroom. A bedroom with an en suite bathroom also adds a touch of luxury: it's good to be able to pamper yourself with your very own facilities, close to dressing and sleeping areas, and to enjoy the privacy of being able to move from one area to another without the bother of putting on clothes and a public face.

Planning ahead Installing a bathroom involves expense, but it should add value to your house unless you have to lose a bedroom in the process.

In a large home, with bedrooms surplus to normal family needs, replacing a small bedroom with an extra bathroom might well enhance the desirability of the property, as well as being of benefit to the current occupants. Otherwise it may be a better investment to spend a little more in the first place to achieve the optimum compromise of bedroom and bathroom.

To avoid losing a bedroom, consider moving a shared wall to take space from two adjoining bedrooms. If you have to reconcile yourself to positioning the new bathroom completely within your bedroom, there are several ingenious systems that provide bathroom facilities for tiny areas. Even a simple shower cubicle in a bedroom corner will help relieve the morning queue.

It's important to get advice from a qualified plumber from the outset. To keep down costs, make use of existing plumbing as far as you are able. Plumbing additions or alterations must comply with water by-laws, and changes to the waste system have to conform to building regulations: your local authority will be able to advise.

En suite scene
A modern en suite bathroom needn't be bleakly functional: this one handsomely picks up the style and period feel of the adjoining bedroom. The rich red in the sumptuous fabrics around the bed is repeated on chairs in both areas and on the bathroom walls.

▽ **Cover story**
If you don't want jarringly functional equipment in the corner of a pretty bedroom, blend in the new installation by running wallpaper over cupboard doors as well as walls so that fitments merge smoothly into the bedroom scene. The basin here is a restful pastel shade; pink tones are emphasized in accessories.

INITIAL PLANNING

At the outset you will need to take advice on the best positioning of sanitaryware in relation to existing plumbing. Fitting bulky equipment into a small space is quite a challenge, especially as you won't be able to move things once they're installed. Some manufacturers' brochures have cut-out scale drawings of basic equipment, which you use with a plan to get an accurate idea of positionings. Remember to leave enough space to use each facility in comfort and safety.

It's worthwhile ensuring everything, including labour, is the best you can afford. Poor installation could lead to damp and condensation problems.

Ventilation should be planned at the start. An opening window could be draughty so consider instead an extractor fan fitted to an exterior wall or window. If the new bathroom is completely internal, you *must* fit an extractor. Fans for internal rooms can switch on with the light or operate when the humidity rises above a pre-set level.

FINDING THE SPACE

En suite ensemble If you aren't able to borrow space from an adjoining room, you will have to install your new amenities in an area of the bedroom. One possible arrangement is to run a false wall the full length of the room which may give space for clothes storage as well as bathroom basics.

For a small bedroom consider either a shower cubicle, possibly with WC from the same range, or a minute cabin-style bathroom that fits neatly into a corner, taking up only 1.35m on each wall. The basic kit consists of an enclosure with sanitaryware and fittings; the unit base converts to a bath.

The only solution in a really tiny room, if you are determined to have extra facilities, is a wash basin/shower unit with a fold-away tray that takes up very little space when not in use.

SPACE SAVERS

Look for ideas that give maximum amenities in a small area.

Showers can be above-bath. A separate cubicle takes up less than one metre. Doors can open to the right or left. Space-saving doors slide, fold or pivot. Non-standard enclosures will fit below a sloping ceiling or in a dormer.

Baths Compact or sit-up tubs available. Small corner bath may suit some layouts. Bath-cabins have WC and shower.

Basins Wall-hung basins free more floor space; a vanity unit provides storage. A tiny bowl isn't ideal for general use.

A WC that's wall-hung or close-coupled gives more floor space. Consider slim-line or built-in cisterns. Waste can be pumped away through small-bore pipes if position of the soil stack is a problem.

Bidets may be wall-hung or can even roll out from under a basin fitment.

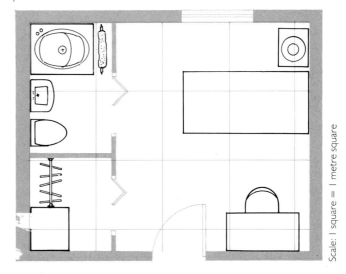

Scale: 1 square = 1 metre square

△ Cupboard fitting
Wooden louvred doors which blend easily with existing bedroom furnishings have been used here to convert a comparatively small area of a bedroom into a trim shower room. The space over the doors could be used for long-term storage.

▷ En suite store
In an alternative arrangement to the one shown above, a line of cupboards has been run along the entire length of the wall. This gives room for a walk-in clothes storage area as well as a WC and soak tub with shower over. A quiet flush WC will allow a nearby sleeper to doze undisturbed. The plan shows the complete layout.

△ ▷ Master suite

If space isn't a problem, a gracious bed
and bath suite can be devised which is
as pleasing on the eye as it must be
pleasurable to use. Some manufacturers
offer a range of matching furnishings for
bed and bath areas – the room shown
on the right has been designed to be a
natural extension of the bedroom. Even
the bath panelling has a similar moulding
to that on the cupboard doors in the
bedroom. Details such as gentle pastels
and soft rugs in both rooms complete
the scene of tranquil luxury. Opaque
glazed doors ensure a degree of privacy
but give en suite continuity.

If you're working to a smaller scale,
adapt some of the ideas for a luxury
finish. Woodwork can be dragged in
both areas, and consider using the same
fabric at windows, behind glazed
cupboards and to conceal the shower –
you can hang waterproof shower
curtains on the inside (see page 16).

▷ *Different functions*
*This modern en suite bathroom shows
how the two areas can share decorative
ideas to give a sense of unity, although
quite different atmospheres can be
created in keeping with the separate
functions. Lighting is particularly
important to set a mood: here the
bedside lamp softly illuminates the
sleeping area. A wall-hung basin can
have plumbing and fixings housed in a
unit to provide storage as well as giving
a streamlined look.*

SEPARATE QUARTERS

An ideal solution to finding space for an
en suite bathroom would be to adapt
an adjacent small bedroom. This may
well allow you to go beyond the basics:
you could include a bidet in your
scheme, and a comfortable chair to
relax in.

If you don't want to lose a bedroom,
a compromise would be to install the
new bathroom between two bedrooms, taking space from each but
ensuring both rooms are still big enough
to function as bedrooms. Remember
always to get expert advice on plumbing and major structural alterations.

DOWN TO DETAILS

Sanitaryware comes in a wide range of
colours and styles. Dark-hued baths and
basins aren't the easiest to keep clean if
the water is hard. If you want a cast-iron
bath, check the floor is sturdy enough to
take the weight. Wall-hung equipment
like a WC should be well supported on
a stout wall.

Decoration of the new bathroom
should be linked to the bedroom
scheme to give a real en suite feel,
though the bathroom needn't have
identical treatment. If your bedroom
has muted, restful tones you could pick
out an accent colour to give a livelier,
refreshing note to the bathroom, perhaps by introducing a little colour and
excitement to accessories like towels.

Wallcoverings will need to cope with
moisture: if the bathroom is tiny,
complete tiling may be possible.

Flooring If you want to carry through
carpeting from the bedroom, protect
damp areas with a mat. Otherwise
choose tiles to blend with the bedroom
floor.

▷ *Arched elegance*
*An adjoining room is linked with an arch
to provide en suite space. Cool
aquamarine tones feature throughout,
especially on the practical part-tiling by
the sanitary fittings. Bathroom curtains
and the bed valance have been made in
the same fabric, with accessories picked
out in toning shades.*

△ **Curved cubicle**
Some shower units are designed to fit neatly into a corner of a room. Different shapes are available, to suit particular layouts; you can even get non-standard housing to fit round awkward shapes.

◁ **Tailored to suit**
Where space is tight it's worth seeking out storage designed to fit round sanitaryware. These units allow you to build up high with lean cupboards.

ELECTRICAL POINTS

Safety must come first in your plans. If you've taken space from a bedroom, have any wall sockets removed as the only socket you can have in a bathroom is a low-voltage shaving point. Take expert advice on electrical installations.

Lighting must be altered if you're using what was a bedroom: a ceiling rose must be replaced with batten holders, and light fittings have to be enclosed. The switch should either be a pull-cord, or be fitted outside the actual bathroom area. Have a general diffused light, with task lighting by the mirror for shaving and making-up.

Heating is important; there's nothing so drear as a chilly bathroom. Look for special bathroom radiators or a heated towel rail. A wall-mounted heater should never be hung above a bath or within splashing range. Don't take portable electric appliances like a fire or hair-drier into the bathroom.

◁ **Bold bathroom**
This bathroom has more dramatic treatment than the bedroom, but colours have been chosen to give a unifying effect. A folding door separates the areas without taking up much space.

You can leave toiletries on display in your en suite, which isn't usually possible in a family bathroom.

THE FITNESS BATHROOM

Exercise your way to good health in the comfort of your home.

Until quite recently anyone doing regular workouts was dubbed a fitness fanatic or health freak. Not so today: we're all much more aware of the need to take care of our bodies. There's been a boom in health clubs which offer everything from pampering steamrooms to punishing circuit training. But regular visits can be expensive and involve quite a commitment – and not everyone wants to pump iron in public!

An alternative is to install your own health centre at home. The preliminary cost may be substantial: if you want anything but the simplest equipment, there's bound to be quite a lot of structural investigation, if not actual alteration, to be done. However you'll have the benefit of taking exercise when you want with equipment to suit your needs.

Space for fitness If you're really keen and can find the space, you'll want the whole works – a mini gymnasium with workbench, wallbars, fitness machines, whirlpool bath, perhaps a sauna. On this scale you may need specialist advice, as you'll almost certainly have to adapt a spare room, take over a second bathroom or even abandon the bathroom completely and convert space at the back of the garage.

More modest schemes could include exercise equipment that folds away: some quite sophisticated systems stack flat against a wall. Take a long look at your bathroom and surrounding area. Would high-level storage release floor space? Maybe there's a landing area you can draw into use by moving a wall. If space is tight consider replacing a bath with a power shower, and fitness equipment that folds for easy storage.

Health combination
Installing a shower rather than a bath in a second bathroom may give enough space for exercise equipment. You can end your workout with an invigorating shower – this cubicle comes packed flat for home assembly.

◁ **Bubble bath**
Bathtime is invigorating for children and adults alike with an airbath that gives adjustable degrees of turbulence. Heated air is pumped from small jets in the base of the bath, allowing you either to relax in gently massaging bubbles or submit yourself to energetic pummelling.

▽ **Steaming up**
After your workout, ease those tired muscles in the comfort of a steam enclosure. As well as a shower head this one has retractable seating, recessed downlighters – and you can even fit moisture-proof loudspeakers and relax to the gentle strains of music.

WATER TREATS

A whirlpool bath is pleasantly relaxing and may give temporary relief to arthritic or rheumatic joints, but take medical advice before using a whirlpool if you're pregnant or have a kidney complaint. If you're unsure what you want, some suppliers will let you try out different systems.

All whirlpool effects involve electric pumps so for safety's sake consider only specialist equipment and installation. Some pumps make quite a racket so listen before you buy.

There are two main systems – the whirlpool jet (such as the Jacuzzi) recirculates bath water mixed with air through outlets on the bath sides. The direction of the jet is adjustable. With the second system – air or spa baths – air is forced into the water through holes in the base and the backrest of the bath.

Whirlpools aren't cheap. If your bath is in good condition, a whirlpool effect can be added: air can be pumped through specially-drilled outlets or forced through holes in a special mat.

Health showers Power showers with a multi-function shower head give a soft or torrent spray or invigorating needle jet. There are also massage shower heads or for all-over action a special frame gives a series of side jets.

A steam shower may be ideal in a spare room or landing space, as a steam-only system doesn't need to be plumbed in unless you want an ordinary shower, too. Shower rooms and enclosures with full plumbing are both also available.

Saunas A good-sized home sauna seats four or five; the cabin of a small sauna, seating two, is about 130cm square. As well as bench and headrests, the cabin has a stove – usually electric nowadays, though wood-burners are available – heat retaining rocks, a bucket and ladle, thermometer and light.

Assembly of a sauna kit isn't too arduous. No plumbing is required, but you need a power supply – use a pull cord if the sauna is in a bathroom – and an opening window or extractor fan. Let a cold shower substitute for the traditional roll in the snow.

Before installing a sauna, have a medical checkup as intense heat can aggravate some conditions. Limit the time you spend in the sauna, initially.

◁ **Steam machine**
Steam treatment relaxes and refreshes a tired body. This attractive hexagonal cubicle has a seat so you can become steamed up at your leisure. A special unit generates steam at a pre-selected temperature for up to two hours.

△ **Heat treat**
A sauna is great for reviving a tired system, and it needn't take up too much space. This little cabin, custom-built to fit into an ordinary bathroom, uses the bath as a plunge pool so the really hardy can take a bracing cold dip.

BRIGHT IDEA

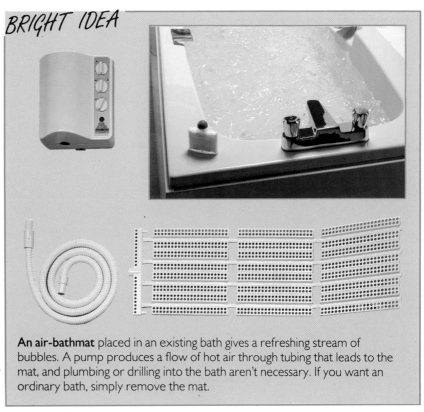

An air-bathmat placed in an existing bath gives a refreshing stream of bubbles. A pump produces a flow of hot air through tubing that leads to the mat, and plumbing or drilling into the bath aren't necessary. If you want an ordinary bath, simply remove the mat.

EQUIPPED FOR FITNESS

For a general programme to increase well-being, aim for a balance of three main elements: aerobic exercise such as cycling, rowing or jogging; body toning – spot exercising of one specific area, perhaps with weights; and relaxation/ water treatment – a whirlpool bath, steam shower or sauna. Draw up a realistic timetable for your routine, and stick to it – the most elaborate and expensive gear won't get you in good shape if it's hardly touched.

To find exercise apparatus to suit your needs and the available space, shop around and try out as much as you can. Allow plenty of activity space in your initial calculations, and consider where apparatus will be stored so that it doesn't get in the way. Home fitness manufacturers are aware of space contraints in the average bathroom: there are plenty of fold-away and wall-mounted systems on the market.

Equipment ranges from a complete workout system for serious exercise to a folding bike in a corner of the room. For the enthusiast without much space, a multi-trainer with bench and wallbars adapts for a variety of exercises and stacks against a wall after the workout.

If you shudder at the thought of anything rigorous, like an abdominal crunch press, why not spring into shape with one of the jolliest ideas on the market – a mini-trampoline, or re-bounder, on which you develop a nice rhythm while bouncing or skipping.

More conventional, and the most popular home exercise machine, is an exercise bike: some convert to a rowing action. Look for a bike with enclosed drive chain and smooth, quiet operation. On some the resistance can be increased for more strenuous exercise. Fit a book clamp and catch up with some reading while you pedal your way to fitness.

△ ◁ *Activity bathroom*
The facilities of a fitness centre can be combined with the pleasures of a luxury bathroom: there's a whirlpool to refresh the spirit and ease tired muscles after exercising. A special storage panel on the bath holds weights or toiletries, and there's even a shelf for your waterproof, battery-operated personal stereo.

A space-saving idea (shown in the view on the left) is the massage/sun deck that folds flat against the wall to give access to the bath. The solarium canopy over the bath is raised and lowered at the touch of a button and stored near the ceiling. Always wear goggles, and follow manufacturer's instructions, when using a solarium.

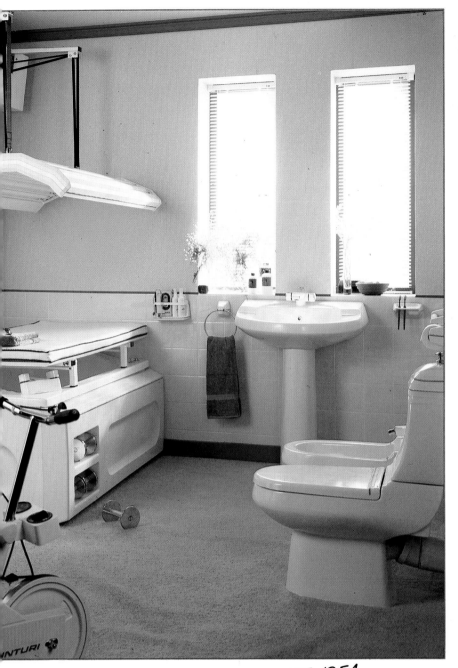

△ **Wall workout**
A wall-mounted home multi-exerciser with bench and wallbars can be used by several members of the family as it adapts for a variety of exercises to suit different levels of fitness. After use it all folds away to stack neatly against the wall.

When installing this sort of equipment make sure you attach it very securely to a wall – and floor – that's sturdy enough to take the strain.

BRIGHT IDEA

A special exercise mat is a sensible idea for a regular routine: apart from giving a soft base for your workout, a mat reduces noise and vibration and also protects floorcoverings from excessive wear. A carry strap holds the rolled mat neatly in place when it is not in use.

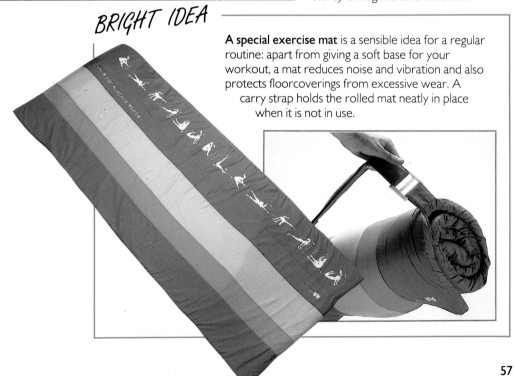

SAFELY FIT

Have a medical checkup before exercising if you're unfit or not in the best of health. Don't take too energetically to a new routine: go gently at first.

Never exercise just after a meal – allow at least two hours for food to digest – or when you're tired. If you feel any pain, stop immediately.

Exercise regularly, three or four times a week for twenty to thirty minutes, in a warm, well-ventilated room.

Wear comfortable clothing that doesn't restrict circulation, and breathe as normally as possible while doing your routine.

Use gentle stretch exercises to warm up and cool down before and after your workout.

Use equipment according to manufacturer's instructions: make sure it's stored safely after use, particularly if there are small children around.

Allow plenty of room to use everything safely – don't underestimate how much space something like dumb-bells or a skipping rope need.

△ **Pedal power**
An exercise bike is one of the most popular home exercise machines as it needs no special installation and adapts easily for different degrees of fitness. Look for one with a low centre of gravity for stability.

▽ **Heavy metal**
A dumb-bell set with ten weights has an attractive yet tough cover to keep you and your bathroom looking neatly trim. This set has a special screw fitting for quick weight changes.

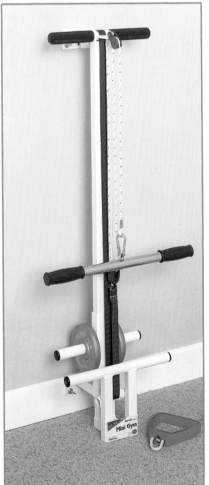

◁ **Home health**
A mini-gym that quickly fits on wall plates or in a doorway can be used for up to thirty different exercises. It's quiet in operation, so would be ideal for an upstairs bathroom or flat.

CREATIVE BATHROOM TILING
For the adventurous, imaginative use of tiling will add flair and originality to your bathroom.

Ceramic tiles have long been recognized as one of the most practical surfaces for a bathroom, particularly in areas likely to come into contact with water. For practical reasons, it's a sound proposition to half- or fully-tile a bathroom wall as well as tiling the casing and surrounds of fitments such as bath and basin.

Much modern tiling is of course pleasing to the eye as well as practical, and in recent years the options for creative use of tiling have rapidly expanded. For the adventurous, this wide range of tiles presents a challenge to put creativity to work on designing a tiling effect uniquely suited to individual bathroom requirements and personal taste.

There certainly is no shortage of possibilities, with a splendid array of vibrant colours and unusual shapes, such as diamond, hexagonal and octagonal. The actual surface of a tile can be plain, raised, embossed, or incised. Patterns range from the prettily floral to modern geometric designs, with some also borrowing inspiration from a past era – there are many good copies of Victorian and Edwardian styles. Others, for example the high tech metallic finishes, are distinctly futuristic. Mural tiles or richly-decorated tile panels can create a focal point, and a range of attractive borders adds to the possibilities of creative tiling.

Before you let your imagination run riot, however, you must first sort out the practicalities. Start your initial planning by examining the shape and size of your room. Clever tiling can help to conceal flaws and highlight strengths. Which areas do you want to enhance, which encourage to fade into the background?

You must also study the surfaces. Are the walls square? Tiles produce such a perfect grid that flaws can be obvious. Use a spirit level to trace any fault, and plan so that a row of cut tiles falls in the least obvious place.

With such a wealth of ideas to choose from, remember mistakes can be costly. Spend time planning your tiling designs; it's too late to change your mind once the tiles are finally up. When looking for inspiration, find pictures of finished rooms, rather than making decisions based on a small section of tiling: what can be pleasing in small measure may be overpowering on four walls.

Draw on graph paper a plan of the walls and tile positioning; pin this up, with variations, in your bathroom and live with the idea for a while, until you are quite certain about your choice.

If you are using standard-sized tiles and your design is complex, invest in a grid which fixes to the wall, providing a framework for arranging and rearranging the design so you can see the result before you finally cement your tiles in place. Alternatively, lay the tiles down on a large flat surface to check the positioning.

Plain and patterned
A combination of different small, chunky tiles has been grouped to provide an attractive patchwork effect around a wash area. Note how they have been symmetrically arranged to give an unobtrusive sense of order to the overall design.

△ **Linear point**
An attractive and inexpensive way to add a dash of colour to budget-priced plain tiles is to use coloured grouting. The same colour can accent other features of the bathroom: here bold lines of red pull together different aspects of a room which, without special treatment, could have remained nondescript.

◁ **Tiling partners**
Two complementary methods of finishing off a panel of plain tiles: a pretty floral border echoes wall and curtain pattern, while a top layer gives a neat zigzag finish. If you want to create a similar effect, take care when cutting diagonals to ensure they are the same size as the square tiles, as a diagonal cut through the centre will obviously be longer than the outside edge.

MAINLY PLAIN

Very handsome effects can be produced by imaginative use of plain tiles, either on their own or combined with more decorative styles. Ordinary whites and neutrals are generally less expensive than vivid hues, but if you are tempted by anything particularly vibrant make quite sure you won't tire of the result after a while.

Tiles can be prohibitively expensive. If you want to keep costs down, consider budget-priced plain tiles for most of the area with the addition of more extravagant special effects such as borders or decorative inserts of single tiles, panels or even a tiled mural. Remember, though, if you use tiles from different ranges make sure they are of equal thickness.

With clever positioning, plain tiles on their own are subtly pleasing. Square and rectangular tiles can be laid stepped, in bricklaying fashion, while square tiles laid diagonally look handsome — they often create a more spacious effect than those laid in the conventional, straight method.

For good looks at low cost, consider using coloured grouting with budget-priced plain tiles which gives a very effective fine grid of colour. Grouting can be bought in a range of colours, or you can buy pigment if you want to colour it yourself.

△ **Blue mood**
Overall tiling in deep colours can produce dramatic impact, but to avoid too dense a result introduce variations on your theme. Here different tones of vibrant blue tiles are laid diagonally on walls but conventionally straight on other surfaces to add interest.

◁ **Tiled panels**
As an alternative to the overall scheme of rich blue tiles pictured above, a more neutral background can be used to give a lighter result, with the addition of distinctive panels and borders. The panels, large or small, can be designed to suit the size and shape of your room.

BORDER STORY

One of the most attractive ideas to give a fine finish to tiling is through introducing a border. These can range from delicate bands of fine pattern to bold, wide friezes. Borders can be added at ceiling or dado level, or can round off a partly-tiled surface.

Running a border or frieze around the room at dado height can help draw together aspects of an awkwardly-shaped room, and may give an impression of more pleasing proportions. A border can also frame attractive features – a pretty mirror, perhaps, or a window.

Tiles specifically designed as borders are frequently manufactured to complement a whole tiling range. They are often narrow rectangles, flat or raised. Modern versions of Victorian dado tiles are available, with the tiles ending in a raised sill.

You could experiment by creating your own borders. Coloured or patterned tiles can border contrasting styles, or you can build up a chequerboard effect with coloured tiles. The cumulative effect of a broad band of several rows can be dramatic, or consider swooping diagonal patterns across a large field of tiles on one or more walls. These more original creative ideas can give a great deal of satisfaction, but they do need conviction and careful thinking through at the planning stage before you commit yourself to any expenditure.

△ **Sunny spots**
Splashes of yellow on tiling and accessories cheer the starkness of pristine white. Note how disparate elements can be drawn together through careful use of accent colour.

▷ **Simply classic**
A subtle variation in tile positioning: large off-white wall tiles are stepped in brick fashion rather than laid conventionally in straight vertical rows. A black and white chequered border adds interest at dado level, and white floor tiles bordered by black complete the sophisticated effect.

◁ Tiling trim
As well as breaking up plain runs of tiling, contrasting colours or patterns can be used to draw the eye towards focal points in the bathroom. Here a mock dado in white and pink is extended to border the mirror, making a pretty feature of the area.

▽ Plain and pattern
There is a wide variety of different plain and patterned tiles on the market which can be arranged to suit your individual specifications. In this alternative arrangement of the wash-basin area pictured left, the tile section under the mock dado has a trellis pattern. The floral-edged border is also used to frame a mirror.

▽ Dashing dado
To relieve a large, bland stretch of tiling, decorative tiles can be added to provide interest at dado height. This border undulates round the room adding a cheerful dash to an otherwise muted colour scheme.

Diagonal tiling can add a subtle dimension to plain tiles. Blocks of diagonals bordered by rows of straight tiling can create stylish geometric patterning.

Tiles laid on the diagonal take up more space than those laid straight, so work out the positioning of adjacent diagonal and straight tiles carefully. Plot the whole panel on squared paper before you start. If necessary, trim the centre tile, as shown above, for a neat finish.

△ *Tiling framework*
Clever positioning of plain tiles can produce a very distinguished result. Here a window with a blind is made a decorative feature by skilful use of a soft green tiled surround – the tiles are built up above the window to form a handsome centrepiece within the framework provided by the gently contrasting wall.

Elsewhere in the same room the effect of long stretches of floor-to-ceiling tiling on facing walls is partly relieved by an ornate bamboo frame and decorative fan.

△ *Proud border*
Attractive raised borders can be used to create a dado on a plain run of tiles, or to highlight points of interest in a bathroom. This border is available in a range of subtle colours.

▷ *Fitment details*
A novel way of introducing pattern to plain tiled walls: these stylish tiling details make a decorative feature of bathroom fitments such as towel hooks and soap dishes.

BOXING IN THE SIDES OF BATHS

You can give your bathroom a new look by changing the panelling down the side of the bath – or create a luxurious and dramatic effect with a new surround.

Modern baths come complete with moulded panels that clip into place to hide the underside of the bath, and the supply and waste pipes. They are convenient and easy to fit, but may not fit in with your decor. In older homes, there may be problems. Flimsy hardboard panels round the sides of the bath may have deteriorated, or perhaps you want to change an existing panel.

You can buy matching shaped plastic or glass fibre side and end panels for almost every modern bath these days. And there are even curved panels to cope with corner baths. However, if you want to decorate the sides of your bath enclosure in some other way, you can achieve dramatic effects by boxing in the side yourself.

The principle is the same, whatever material you choose to use for the cladding and decoration. You start by building a simple framework of soft-wood posts and rails along the sides and end of the bath, and then attach the cladding material to this.

CHOOSING A FINISH
The cladding material can either be a finish in itself, or a surface to which you can add your chosen finish. For example, a purpose-designed mahogany panel or an old pine door can be fitted round the sides of a bath for a traditional look. For a more rustic effect, tongued-and-grooved boards, either varnished or painted, are a suitable choice. If your bathroom has a carpeted floor, you can even run the carpet up the side of the bath, though a better choice might be sheet vinyl to match existing flooring, or ceramic tiles to match the bath surround.

You could use hardboard if you plan to paper the panels, but the best bet (and the only choice if you want to tile the panels) is plywood. Don't use chipboard in a bathroom because it swells and bursts if it gets wet. For the same reason, any hardboard you use should be the oil-tempered variety, and plywood should be at least moisture-resistant (MR) grade. Ideally, water and boil-proof (WBP) board should be chosen.

ALLOWING FOR ACCESS
A vital point to bear in mind when boxing anything in, is that you might need access to it at some time in the future. For example, you may need to get at the waste trap of a bath if you have a blockage. If you think about this point at the planning stage, it's generally a simple matter either to make the panelling easy to remove, or to incorporate some sort of access hatch.

Tiled panel
This bath has been boxed in with a plywood panel which has then been tiled over. Similar panels are built in at the end and side of the room.

PLANNING THE JOB

Once you have decided that you want to panel in your bath and what type of finish you want on the panel, you have to start planning the job in a little more detail. It is simplest to fit a panel flush with the side of the bath, but if you have the space and have some experience of woodwork, it is attractive to build a shelf at the same time as the panelling, so that the panel is about 15cm out from the side of the bath. You need to measure up the bath so you can sketch out the framework and work out how much timber you'll need for it, what sized cladding panels will be required, and how you will make the various fixings.

HALVING JOINTS

To make up the framework supporting the bath panel described in this chapter you have to make a fairly simple joint, called a halving joint. It is used when you want to make a T-shaped join between two pieces of timber.

1 *Measure and mark the joint* ▷
In this example, the rebate to be cut is 25mm×25mm, set into a 50mm square batten. Using a try square, mark round three sides of the batten, 25mm from the top. Mark across the top and down the sides, 25mm from the front.

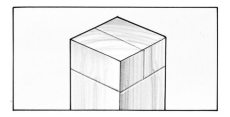

2 *Make the first cut* ▷
Set the batten upright in a workbench and use a tenon saw to saw down from the top, following the marked line, until you reach the line marked round the batten. It is very important that both the pencil marks and the saw cut are accurate, to get a good fit and a perfect right angle.

3 *Make the second cut*
Turn the batten on its side, so it protrudes from the end of the workbench and saw downwards, following the line marked across the batten, until you meet the previous cut and the waste block of wood comes out.

4 *Screwing the joint together* ▷ ▷
Offer up the batten to be set into the joint you have made, and check the fit. Chisel or saw away any surfaces which stand proud. Mark screw positions so they are staggered (to avoid splitting the wood). Remove the batten and drill clearance holes through the batten, plus countersunk holes for the heads of the screws. Offer up the batten again, and use a bradawl to mark the other half of the joints. Use a fine drill to make pilot holes a few millimetres into the cut half of the joint. Apply woodworking adhesive to all parts of the joint which meet. Position the batten and screw firmly in place.

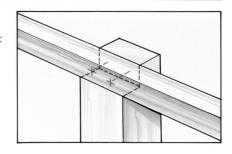

SKEW NAILING

This is a useful technique for making a T-shaped joint between fairly substantial battens (in this case 25×50mm and 50mm square). It is a quick and easy fixing method, but should only be used where the joint is to be covered (inside a stud wall, or behind a bath panel, for example). Also, it is only suitable if the other end of the upright part of the T is to be firmly fixed. In the situation where skew nailing is used here (under the bath) the cross bar of the T-joint is fixed firmly to the floor first.

1 *Position the upright* ▷
Set the upright on the cross bar and use a pencil to mark its position (so you can ensure it is still in the right place when the nailing is finished). Temporarily nail an offcut of wood so that one edge of it butts up to the upright. (Cramp it in place rather than nailing, if this is possible.)
Using a 75mm oval wire nail, drive it in at an angle through the upright, into the cross piece, positioning it about a third of the way across the width of the battens – in this case, about 15mm in from the front edges of the two battens to be joined. (Oval nails are used to prevent the wood from splitting.)

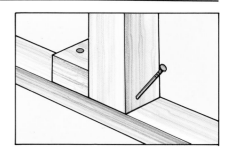

2 *Nail in the other direction*
Remove the offcut of wood, and re-nail it on the other side of the joint. Drive in a second nail from the other side, positioning it so that it is two-thirds of the way across the joint (ie the nails are evenly spaced across the joint).

FITTING A BATH PANEL

The framework can be made of sawn timber (rather than better-looking and more expensive planed all round [par] type). As with all carpentry work, it is important to plan the work carefully before you start and make accurate measurements at each stage. These instructions are for fitting a side *and* end panel, with adjustments for fitting a side panel where appropriate.

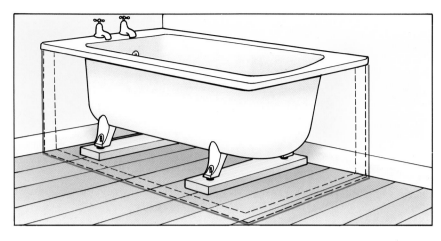

1 Measure round the bath
Start by measuring the length of each panel, and decide on the positions of the support battens. Check that there will be no problems fixing them in place (poor plasterwork, missing floorboards, etc) and make good if necessary. You will probably need a batten fixed to the wall at each end of the area to be panelled, two battens down the side and one at the corner (if appropriate).

2 Cut timber for bottom rails △
Calculate the exact length of each of the bottom rails: subtract the thickness of the cladding material, plus any decorative finish, from each measurement, and subtract 50mm from the width of the bath to give the measurement of the end rail (to accommodate the width of the side rail). (There is no need to subtract anything from the measurement of the length of the bath if you are fitting a side panel only.) Cut two pieces of 50 × 25mm softwood for bottom rails.

3 Fix bottom rails ▷
Lay the rails on the floor directly beneath (and parallel to) the lip of the bath, checking their alignment with a spirit level if necessary. Mark their positions with pencil lines. Now set them back from the marked lines by the thickness of cladding material plus any decorative finish (eg tiles), to allow the panel to finish neatly below the bath lip. Nail the battens to a wooden floor (beware of pipes running too close to the surface), or plug and screw them in place if the bath is on a solid floor.

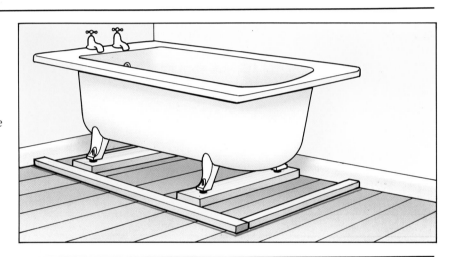

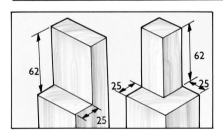

4 Measure and cut uprights △
Then measure the distance between the underside of the bath, up underneath the lip, and the top edge of the floor battens. Cut pieces of 50mm square wood to this length plus 2mm for the uprights; you'll need four to panel in a bath side, or five if you are panelling an end as well. Following the instructions opposite, use your tenon saw to cut out a 62mm×25mm halving joint at one end of each post, ready to accept the 50×25mm top rail later (the extra 12mm is to allow for any overhang of the bath lip). Cut the halving both ways on the corner post if you are also doing the end of the bath.

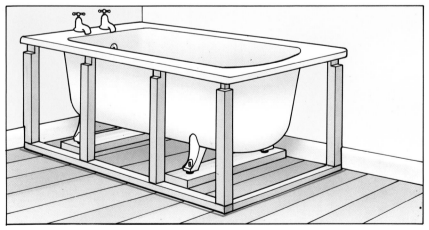

5 Fit the uprights △
Wedge the posts into place between the floor battens and the bath lip, with the halvings at the top, facing out into the room. For two panels, position one post against each wall at the ends of the long and short panels, one at the corner and two more equally spaced down the long side of the bath. (For a single panel you should position one upright against the wall at each end, with the other two equally spaced between.) Scribe the end posts to fit round the skirting if necessary. The extra 2mm in length should ensure that they are a tight fit. Check that they are vertical in each direction using your spirit level. Then skew-nail their feet to the floor battens, and screw the two end battens to the walls.

6 Position top rails
Measure and cut to length the
50×25mm top rail(s) to match the
bottom rail(s). Offer them up into the
halvings you cut in the tops of the posts,
drill clearance and countersinking holes,
and glue and screw them to the tops of
the posts. If you try to nail them, you
risk knocking the posts out of alignment.

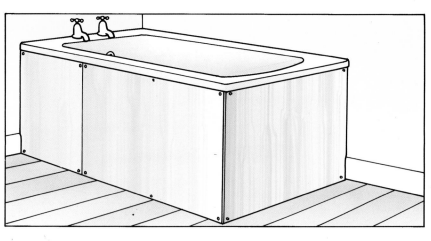

7 Fit cladding panels ▷
Measure up for each cladding panel
and cut it to size. If you are fitting two
panels, remember to add the thickness
of the cladding to the lengthwise
measurement to get a neat finish at the
corner. You may need to divide the
side panel into two sections to get
access to the waste trap: this will
depend on the nature of the cladding
material. A single mahogany panel, for
example, can be fitted with six mirror
screws, so that the whole panel is
removed for access. On the other hand,
if the panel is to be tiled, you only want
a small access panel, so split the side
panel into two parts, one to fit the 'bay'
between the first two posts at the tap
end of the bath, the other to fit the rest
of the bath side. Then offer up each

panel to the framework and scribe the
ends to fit round skirtings if necessary.
Drill pilot and countersinking holes
along each edge of the larger panel at
around 400-500mm intervals and screw
the panel to the framework. Fix the
smaller panel with mirror screws drilling
pilot holes first. Do not fit the
decorative heads on mirror screws at
this point, and do not tighten them if
you are planning to tile the panels.

8 Apply finish
If the cladding is to be decorated,
seal it with a coat of size ready for
papering (a vinyl wallcovering is best in a
bathroom), or with a coat of diluted
PVA adhesive if you plan to tile it. Paper
over mirror screws, then replace their
decorative heads. If you are tiling the
removable access panel, remove each
corner screw and drill through the tile
that will cover it at the appropriate
point with a masonry drill. Then fix the
tile in position, drive the screws back in
and fit the decorative heads.

FITTING A PANEL AND SURROUND

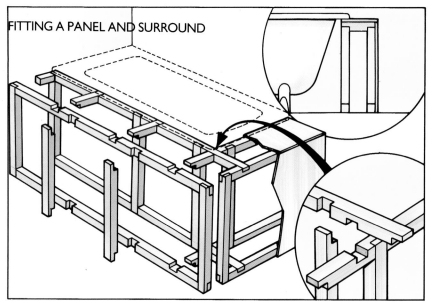

◁ Building the framework
The framework for a panelled bath with
a shelf surrounding the edge of the bath
has to be slightly more substantial than
for a straight panel. Use 50mm square
timber with halving joints as indicated.
Measure and cut all the joints first. All
the uprights are the same length as the
finished height of the box, less the
thickness of the cladding material (see
inset, top right). Halving joints are cut at
each end of the uprights, facing inwards
to make fixing easier. Cut halving
recesses in the horizontal elements of
the framework to accept the uprights
and the cross struts at the top used to
support the cladding. At the corner, the
two inner horizontal struts interlock to
make a firm joint (see inset, bottom
right).

▷ Bathroom luxury
If you can spare the room, a 'peninsular'
bath with a wide surround creates a
really luxurious effect. In a less spacious
room, you can still add the surround on
two sides to provide a shelf for
ornaments and toiletries, without having
to move the bath itself. Note how a
panelled effect has been created by
applying extra wooden strips round the
edge of the panels, tacking and gluing it
in place. Fit mouldings inside the recess
created in this way to give a traditional
air. The panels will have to be
thoroughly sanded and primed before
applying under- and topcoats of paint.

SHOWER ROOMS

When space is tight, fitting a shower room may be the logical alternative to a conventional bathroom.

Showers are more economical than baths – they're quick and easy, they use less hot water and they take up less space. A shower room is also easier and less expensive to install than a bathroom, and children love showers.

The shower There are several different types of shower available, the most common ones being mixer and instantaneous. A mixer shower can be plumbed in from the existing hot and cold water system. The drop from the bottom of the cold water tank to the shower head needs to be at least 90cm to give you

sufficient pressure of water (this distance is known as the 'head'). If the pressure is too low, it may be worth fitting a booster pump or raising the cold water tank.

An instantaneous shower, powered by gas or electricity, takes cold water directly from the mains supply, heating the water while it is running. This type of shower can be very economical because it only heats the water you use, so there is no need for a hot water supply, or even a tank.

Because you can adjust them to the

height of the user, hand held shower heads are more flexible than, but not as neat as, fixed ones. With thermostatic controls, the water temperature is maintained even if other taps in the house are being run – most important in a large family or multi-occupied house. Controls which maintain the pressure of the flow of water are also available.

Cubicles Shower areas need to be fully waterproof. They must be enclosed on two or three sides, with a door or shower curtain on the remaining side(s).

Cubicles come ready-built, but for

Stylish simplicity
This rectangular room could have been fitted with a bath but the owners preferred the idea of a luxurious shower room, using the extra space for twin basins.

The fully tiled shower area has a corner tray. The angle of the pair of frosted glass doors across the entrance is echoed by the diagonal floor tiles.

more versatility, there is a wide selection of self-assembly showers. Made of toughened glass or plastic, these comprise of back and side panels with a choice of corner opening, bi-fold, sliding and curved corner door options. If you want to fit a shower into an oddly shaped space, it is worth considering tiling the entire area, including the floor (using non-slip tiles), and using a shower door or curtain over the entrance.

Shower trays are usually made from ceramic, enamelled steel or acrylic and come in a range of sizes, the most common being 762mm, 815mm and 900mm square, although there are also rectangular and corner models.

Practicalities You need to consider plumbing, safety and ventilation. So ask your local authority about the regulations governing the installation of showers and drainage connections before starting any work.

It is usually fairly straightforward to run water to the shower but connecting the drainage can be more difficult. The length and slope of the waste pipe is not as critical as with a toilet but placing the shower cabinet against an outside wall and near to other plumbing units makes things easier.

Flooring In a shower room, the flooring should be water resistant as well as

△ **Green and yellow**
Co-ordinating vinyl wallcoverings are used above and below the bright green dado rail in this cheerful shower room. Vinyl is ideal in a bath or shower room – it has a thick coating which is water resistant.

The flooring has been chosen for its practicality and good looks. The white tiles are bordered with green for definition. Ceramic tiles do get slippery when wet so it's wise to add a floor rug with a rubber, non-slip backing or underlay.

good looking. There are plenty of choices. Vinyl tiles or cushion flooring is comfortable to stand on and is easily cleaned and there are hundreds of styles and patterns to choose from. Cork tiles sealed with polyurethane varnish are warm and practical and their neutral tones fit in well with most colour schemes. Ceramic tiles are a traditional bathroom or shower flooring; they are beautiful and very hardwearing but are expensive and feel cold and hard.

If, however, you prefer the warmth of carpet, it is best to go for the ridged, rubber-backed kind made specifically for use in bathrooms. Ordinary carpet eventually rots if it is continually splashed with water.

BRIGHT IDEA

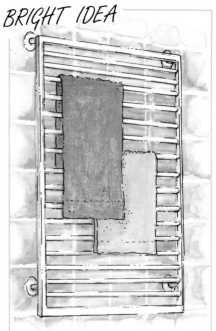

Towel radiator A single heated towel rail is rarely sufficient to heat a bathroom or shower room, while a conventional radiator doesn't give much towel hanging space. An alternative is to fit a stylish towel radiator with horizontal bars, available in a variety of heights.

DECORATION

A shower room has to be practical but there's no reason why it can't look good too – you can use as much imagination here as in any other room in the house. But because it's got to survive splashes of water, wet feet and even the occasional flood, surfaces need to be waterproof and easily dried.

The area inside the shower itself must be totally waterproof. It can be tiled or panelled but make sure that waterproof adhesive and grouting is used for the tiles and any gaps into which water might seep are properly sealed with a flexible sealant.

Outside the shower area, bear in mind that, as well as splashes of water, condensation can be a problem. Wall tiles are ideal but paint, preferably an oil-based one, is an inexpensive alternative as long as the walls are smooth. Gloss or eggshell is scrubbable and stands up well to moisture. If you prefer wallpaper, choose a vinyl or water resistant finish.

This large cloakroom has enough space for a shower enclosure as well as a basin and toilet. The corner opening cubicle is a good choice, ensuring a protected space for the toilet and there is plenty of room for hanging clothes and towels.

Here it is decorated in three very different ways. The basic room remains the same – the walls inside the shower are tiled in white and the plain white sanitaryware is the perfect foil for a variety of colour schemes.

scale: 1 square = 1 metre

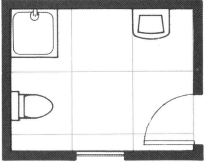

▽ Soft and practical
A striped waterproof wallcovering in soft yellow, peach and grey with a co-ordinating border is teamed with silver grey paintwork.

The area below the dado rail is gloss painted in pale yellow; this is an inexpensive and attractive alternative to tiles. Flooring is honey-coloured cork, sealed to protect it from water staining or seeping through the joins.

◁ Paint effect
Here, the walls are rag rolled in shades of pink for a softer, sophisticated effect, and then protected with several layers of clear matt polyurethane varnish which creates a hard-wearing surface.

The floor is covered with black and white vinyl tiles arranged in a chequered pattern, while the horizontal line detail from the shower cubicle is picked up on the towel radiator (see Bright Idea).

71

FITTING IN A SHOWER

If space is at a premium, it may be worth considering abandoning the idea of a bathtub completely in favour of a shower room in a small house or flat. It is also a compact solution if you want a second bathroom.

A self-contained cubicle takes up barely one square metre of floor space. As well as in the bathroom itself, there are plenty of other places where a shower can be installed: the corner of a bedroom, possibly behind cupboard doors; in an unused alcove; at the end of a corridor; even under the stairs.

It's no good installing a shower into such a tight corner that there's no room outside the cubicle to keep towels or to undress or dry yourself, so allow a minimum of 70cm square close by.

Space Look at the sizes of shower trays and enclosures carefully before buying. It may be tempting to fit a very small one into a tiny area but make sure it is big enough to use comfortably. Don't be afraid to climb inside the enclosure in the showroom to see how it feels.

SAFETY

Water and electricity make dangerous partners but, used properly, can be perfectly safe.

Light bulb holders in bathrooms must have extended covers to avoid the possibility of electric shocks. If fittings are likely to get wet, make sure you choose those which are enclosed. Pull-cord switches are the only safe type to use in a bathroom.

The only sockets you should ever have in a bathroom or shower room are shaver points which have such a low cut-out point that the chance of getting a shock is virtually nil.

Large electical appliances, such as wall heaters or washing machines must be permanently wired into a sealed socket and positioned out of reach of anyone using water.

◁ *Bed into bath*
This L-shaped master bedroom in a converted older house left an unused alcove in the smaller leg. The luxury of an en-suite shower room was the sensible solution.

The colour scheme is a stylish off-white. There is an ivory carpet and the white wall tiles have a shoulder-high border in red and navy blue.

The walls of the shower area are fully tiled and there is a basin in the opposite corner, making maximum use of the available space. The corner cubicle has one solid glass panel with a towel rail fixed to the outside and space-saving sliding doors.

◁ **Under the stairs**
The space under the stairs is often wasted. Not so here, the area neatly houses a shower in what appears to be a tall cupboard. Once the green wooden door is closed, the entire shower cubicle is hidden away.

The wall panels are made of toughened safety glass and the shower door is frosted; while the hall flooring is sensible vinyl.

▽ **Small space solution**
One end of a narrow bedroom has been turned into a tiny shower area. There is just enough space to stand between the vanity unit and the shower tray.

A simple waterproof curtain hangs across the entrance and the walls are covered with textured vinyl.

Hollywood-style strips of bulbs add a touch of glamour – make sure if buying lighting like this that it's suitable for bathroom use.

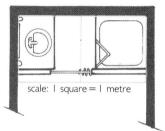

scale: 1 square = 1 metre

SHOWER ROOM STYLE

As shower rooms are usually far from large, colour schemes are best kept simple to help create a feeling of space.

However, decorating a small room does give you the opportunity to be more adventurous or to use more expensive materials than in the main rooms of the house.

◁ *Curtain effect*
Extravagant-looking layers of ruched and frilled curtains turn a simple white shower into a talking point.

This is not quite as impractical as it at first seems. The drapes are made from an easy-care synthetic fabric and underneath is a 'proper' waterproof shower curtain.

△ *Economical choice*
Hiding the plumbing behind a false wall keeps this small space neat. The shower area is completely tiled and the rest of the room is papered with a washable vinyl which picks up the grid pattern of the tiles. A standard basin would leave no room for manoeuvre here, so a narrow space-saving one is used.

▷ *Rug scheme*
The colour scheme for this shower room with a corner cubicle is inspired by the oriental dhurrie rug. The colours used as accents in the rug become the main elements – white floor and sanitaryware and blue tiled walls.

The division between floors and walls is sharply defined by two rows of rust tiles – the strongest colour in the rug.

If you decide to have a floor rug in the shower or bathroom, it is wise to use a non-slip rubber underlay, available from carpet shops or department stores, to avoid accidents.

LOOS AND CLOAKROOMS

A separate loo is a useful addition to most homes – making provision for one can be easier than you think.

For anyone sharing a home with young children, teenagers or elderly people, or regular overnight guests, the advantages of an additional toilet, particularly one downstairs, are self-evident. It relieves congestion during family rush hours and saves children and adults having to climb flights of stairs in a tall house and it also means guests don't ever have to use the main bathroom and can leave their coats downstairs.

More often than not, installing a separate toilet is both feasible and economical; it can even improve the value of your home. But do draw up your plans in consultation with an architect or plumber familiar with local building and water regulations. The installation of a new WC, or any plumbing work that modifies or adds to the existing waste system, must be approved by your local building inspector.

Planning considerations A separate toilet can be fitted into a surprisingly small space. The optimum dimensions of approximately 1400 by 900mm allow room for a standard WC with a 500mm-wide cistern and 700mm projection together with a compact wall-mounted cloakroom hand basin.

Any plans to install a WC depend on the position of the existing soil stack to which it has to be connected via a bulky soil pipe, 100mm in diameter. An ideal situation would be beneath (or above) an existing bathroom, as it is possible to create a further access point to the soil stack at ground floor level, although this is definitely a job for a professional.

The distance from the WC pan to the soil stack should be as short as possible for its gravity-fed drainage system to work efficiently. Sometimes it can be extended by a branch if you decide to put the second WC in a room next to the existing bathroom.

The new small bore units which are connected directly behind the pan enable a WC to be installed almost anywhere in the building, including a basement or attic. Compact and unobtrusive, they incorporate an efficient macerator which finely mills waste on flushing; an electrically-powered pump discharges it through 22mm pipework horizontally to a soil stack up to 20m away. But do bear in mind that this system requires you to have special approval from your local authority before proceeding.

Ventilation A window which opens is not obligatory. But in the absence of one, the Building Regulations demand that ample ventilation be provided by an extractor fan (fitted into a window or an external wall). The extractor can come on automatically together with the light, or be operated by a pull cord linked to the light switch or a simple door-closing mechanism.

Neat and narrow

A separate loo is often confined to a long, narrow space making careful planning and decoration essential.

Here, dark paint helps to lower the high ceiling while bold checks and bright accessories brighten up the room. The cistern is concealed behind a false wall, the top of which acts as a handy bookshelf. A recessed hand basin takes up minimum space.

MAKING THE MOST OF SPACE

As most toilets are small, it's best to choose fittings which use space as economically as possible.

The WC While most WC pans conform to a standard size, cisterns are made in different dimensions. The smallest, generally made of plastic with a top flushing action, is as little as 114mm deep. For a neater toilet, you might opt for the type of WC where the entire cistern is concealed behind a casing about 150mm deep. Wall-hung WCs are another good idea, making a restricted floor area easier to clean.

The basin In a narrow room, a small cloakroom basin is perfectly adequate – some project no more than 150mm into the room with part of the bowl recessed into the wall. In a more generous space, a vanity basin inset into a surround or small storage cupboard is more useful.

Storage Although not essential, making some provision for storage could provide a helpful overspill from overstretched rooms elsewhere in the home. In a standard cloakroom with the toilet at one end, the wall space around the WC might provide a good spot for a variety of shelves and cupboards.

If you are lucky enough to have a downstairs cloakroom it's well worth making provision for hanging coats and hats – either hooks on the wall or door, or a traditional stand with a slot to hold umbrellas. A mirror either above the basin or full-length, perhaps on the back of the door, is a useful addition, especially when it helps to create an illusion of extra space.

▷ *A compact toilet*
In a small toilet such as this one, there is often too little room in front of the WC to install a conventional wash basin. A neat solution is to choose a wall-hung corner basin which takes up very little wall space and leaves the floor area clear.

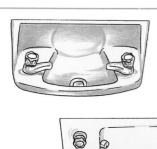

SPACE-SAVING BASINS

All these wall-mounted basins leave the floor area free from plumbing. Those on the left are set into the wall, which must be able to take the recessed part of the basin. The shapes on the right are slightly deeper but are simpler to install. They include a corner sink and one with taps neatly positioned on one side.

▷ Boxed-in

Pipes which run through this room from floor to ceiling on the right of the WC are hidden behind pine panelling, which also includes a set of open shelves. The panelling has been extended to cover the entire back wall and floor.

A turquoise roman blind, towels and accessories liven up the honey-coloured woodwork.

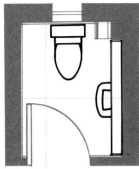

Scale: 1 square = 1 metre square

▽ Pretty pink

A wall-hung WC and basin may involve additional installation work, but they do leave the floor completely free from obstructions. Such streamlined fittings create clean lines in a small room.

▽ ▷ Making space

An alternative way to maximize the amount of free floor space is to install a WC with a narrow cistern, which keeps the entire fitting closer to the wall. To enlarge the room further, a wall-sized mirror topped by recessed downlighters is installed.

CHOOSING A SUITABLE PLACE

In addition to proximity to the soil stack, where you choose to install a loo is limited by the requirement that a room containing a WC must not open directly on to a living room or kitchen and, for obvious reasons, there must be a ventilated lobby in between.

As a hallway can act as a ventilated lobby (providing the doors to the adjoining rooms are left in place), a toilet can be created in the space below the stairs. But first consider its size: while it may conform in length and width to the minimum already mentioned, is it high enough? If the door is to open outwards into the hall, will it clash with other doors close by?

Good ventilation is also necessary. If there is no external wall, it is possible to install a ceiling-mounted extractor fan, provided it can extract into a loft-space above or ducts can connect it to the outside.

Incorporating an outhouse An existing outside toilet at the rear can be incorporated into the structure of the house, providing the ventilated lobby requirement can be met. In older houses which have a toilet beyond the kitchen, there is often a redundant coal shed which can act as the lobby.

A utility room If a utility room adjoins the kitchen, it is sometimes possible to 'poach' a small space to create a downstairs cloakroom. Depending on its size and the appliances housed within it, some judicious doubling up could free the required extra space. Try stacking the tumble dryer on top of the washing machine or investing in a combined washer/drier; sacrificing a chest freezer for a more space-saving upright one; or replacing a large sink with a smaller inset model, smart enough to act as a handbasin, and so on.

Position the WC at·the far end of the room, separated by a partition wall and door, and the reduced-size utility room now acts as the required lobby.

△ *Dual purpose*
This cloakroom serves two roles. As well as taking pressure off the main toilet, it provides the keen gardener with a home for geraniums during winter frosts. The cupboard below the inset basin keeps gardening equipment out of sight.

BRIGHT IDEA

A practical innovation This new-style macerator WC can solve the problem of installing a WC in a place where a connection with the soil stack cannot be made either easily or cheaply. The version which is shown here allows dirty water flowing from a small hand basin to be discharged at the same time as the waste from the WC itself.

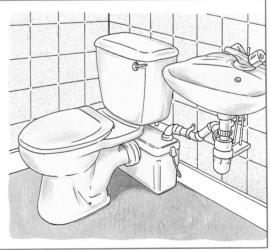

Upstairs Installing an additional loo off a bedroom or on a landing is practical when space permits. If you are planning a bath or shower room en suite to the main bedroom, take into account the location of the existing plumbing. It may be more realistic to switch rooms if another, nearby bedroom allows for easier conversion.

Unlike the previous examples, there are no regulations to prevent you from having a toilet leading directly from a bedroom, but some form of sound-proofing is important. The quietest, though most expensive, syphonic flush WC is a good choice, and wood panelling, carpet and acoustic ceiling tiles help to reduce noise levels, both human and mechanical!

While many homes built during the 1930s have an upstairs toilet separate from the bathroom, many recently-built houses do not. It is, however, often possible to construct a partition wall to separate the WC. If the layout of the bathroom makes it difficult to provide the separate toilet with its own entrance door, consider extending the partition wall only partway along the room. This, at least, provides some privacy if members of the family need to use the bathroom at the same time.

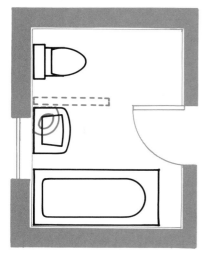

△ *Dividing the bathroom*
If you want to separate the WC from the bath and basin, erecting a partition wall is not difficult. If, as in the plan shown above, creating a separate opening for the toilet would be complicated, consider ending the partition wall part of the way along the length of the room, creating some privacy if not a separate room. A corner sink against the partition helps to make the bathroom area roomier.

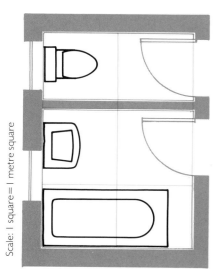

Scale: 1 square = 1 metre square

▽ *Dramatic decor*
Lack of space is turned to advantage in this eye-catching toilet. Blue and yellow vertical stripes are combined with a deckchair-striped, tasselled blind which continues up and across the ceiling. Heavy knotted cords, co-ordinating toilet paper, pompons and woodwork – and two exotic birds complete the stunning effect.

▽ *Shelf space*
A simple way of hiding the WC cistern is to box it in with wooden panels. The top and sides are easy to remove if the cistern requires repairs or maintenance. The wooden box also provides a useful display shelf.

BRIGHT IDEA

A practical sink It's often handy to be able to use a downstairs basin to soak clothes or to fill buckets of water for cleaning floors and washing the car. If there is room, install a deep kitchen sink with a tall mixer tap rather than a small hand basin – modern sinks are made in many attractive bright colours.

△ *Traditional style*
This classically simple room has been furnished with an elegant combination of mahogany woodwork, gleaming taps and a matching blue-and-white inset china hand basin and towel holder.

The WC cistern is built into the back wall of the room, leaving only an unobtrusive flush button visible. When building in a cistern, it is wise to make provision for access to the cistern when it needs mending.

A SIMPLE BATHROOM WITH STYLE

This bathroom is as stylish as it is functional. Neutral backgrounds and extensive use of creamy tiling create a practical co-ordinated scheme, while smooth surfaces conceal generous storage space. Still, it looks far from clinical – filtered light through a simple drape lends warmth to the colour scheme and softens the hard lines of modern fittings.

Cream and white
Pale colours help to create a sense of light and space. Matt cream tiles, fluffy creamy towels and simple white fittings are complemented by touches of gleaming chrome.

A painted wooden moulding forms a neat defining line between wall tiles below and fresh white paint above.

Plant pots
The white flowering plants on the deep windowsill add a touch of green to the cream and white scheme.

The porcelain soup tureen is an attractive alternative to a traditional plant pot – and a good choice for a small space. Several plants can be neatly grouped together and take up little room.

Tiled surfaces
The floor, bath and much of the walls are covered in ceramic tiles for a clean co-ordinated look. Tiles offer excellent resistance to moisture and are easy to maintain, making them ideal for a bathroom.

Never use highly glazed tiles for flooring – they get very slippery when wet. Instead, use non-slip tiles especially designed for bathroom and kitchen use.

Soft and filtered
The white curtain, caught high and tied back, hangs from a white curtain rail. It filters the daylight which floods into the bright room.

Good lighting
Old-fashioned glass ceiling fittings provide diffused general lighting, while a warm fluorescent strip lights up the wash-basin mirror with a golden light – perfectly functional yet not too strong for early morning.

Strip lighting used for shaving and making-up should be wide enough to cast light on the sides of the face as well as the front.

Space-saver
A free-standing towel rack provides lots of hanging space for towels and has the advantage of being movable. In addition, there's a rail underneath the basin countertop on which wet towels can be spread out to dry.

Good storage
The wash-basin alcove is surrounded by streamlined storage units, including a good-sized linen cupboard. Built in a continuous line, the units look neat and uncluttered.

COUNTRY LOOK

A small bathroom with a floral theme. The pale mushroom walls are decorated with blossom motifs taken from the floral patterned fabric used for the ruched austrian blind, while potted plants and cut flowers provide a fresh contrast.

Framed floral prints, wooden shelves and ornamental objects make the room comfortable and extremely cosy.

Flower sprays
Random sprays of blossom on the wall echo the floral print of the blind. These were painted on freehand, but you can achieve a similar effect by stencilling a motif on to the wall.

A frilly blind
The ruched austrian blind, in a charming floral print, is outlined with a frill and sets the scene for the whole room.

Note how the frill is edged with a plum-covered braid which provides style and definition.

Marble top
A plain white basin is set off effectively by an attractive marble surround.

Marble is a classic bathroom luxury – use good-looking imitations, such as Corian, or marble-effect laminates, instead.

Light detail
Brass wall lights with frilled shades suit the pretty floral look of the room.

Hot towels
A towel rail connected to the hot water system heats the bathroom and keeps towels dry and warm at the same time.

You can add a clip-on towel rail to an existing radiator rather than install a special heated rail.

A new face
A new bath panel can give an old fixture a completely new look. Bath panels are available ready-made or you can make your own from boarding enhanced with a rectangle of moulding. This panel has been painted cream, and then dragged with a honey-coloured glaze.

Warm wood
This old-fashioned wooden toilet seat suits the style of the room – it's also warm and more comfortable to sit on than plastic! Wooden toilet seats are available new in either dark or light woods.

Boxed in
In a small room, keep unattractive plumbing out of sight. Here pipes and cistern are neatly hidden behind a panel painted to match the cupboards under the basin. The resulting ledge provides a useful shelf for bottles and ornaments, as well as hand towels.

A BATHROOM IN A NOSTALGIC MOOD

The atmosphere of times past is re-created here but given a new slant with a light and airy scheme which suits modern tastes. A traditional cast-iron bath, brass reproduction taps, an old bamboo folding table and chair are complemented by a pastel scheme.

Display board
A collection of postcards and memorabilia displayed on a pinboard looks just as good in a bathroom as it does in a kitchen, where it is usually found. Colouring the board to match the bath and adding a ribbon trellis in keeping with the room scheme turns a utilitarian idea into an attractive and witty 'picture'.

Brass taps
Choose antique-style taps for a roll-top bath. It is still possible to get old taps from architectural salvage companies. There are also numerous reproductions of period designs on the market.

Posters
Posters are a cheap way to decorate walls and the wide range of designs available makes it possible to find something to suit most situations. Here they are linked to the scheme by their subject and because they have been mounted to match the display board. Ribbon corners give a feeling of a holiday album.

Border detail
Softly patterned walls are an excellent foil for posters and are made more interesting by adding a wallpaper border. Positioning this some way above the bath visually separates the 'business' area of the room from the wall decoration of pinboard and posters.

Furniture and floor
An old lightweight bamboo table and chair, coir matting and a cotton rug give an air of informality which suits the relaxed mood of this light and breezy room.

Stylised shell
The simple single-colour stencilled design on the bath continues the seaside theme set by the travel posters. The fan motif on the border has been modified into a fan-shaped shell.

Old-style bath
You can give an old-fashioned roll-top bath up-to-date chic by painting the outside to fit in with your colour scheme. Add a stencilled design for an individual touch.

Cushions
Cushions are a simple device for giving the finishing touch to a scheme by adding colour, pattern or style accents. Here the stencil motif appears again in satin cushions shaped and quilted to represent shells.

ON A MARINE THEME

In this bathroom the feeling of sea and shore has been created around a modern sand coloured suite.

The walls are lined with tongued-and-grooved boards which have been painted a soft greeny-blue to represent the sea. The carpet has been chosen to pick up the goldy-beige of the suite.

Stencils play a prominent part in this scheme, creating a border of foaming waves around ceiling and skirting and decorating walls with shells and fishes.

Shells and fishes
Stencils in the shape of scallop shells, fishes and waves relieve the solid expanse of colour on the walls.

Colours as well as motifs evoke the sea and shore. Shells and fishes are in a similar sandy shade to that of the bathroom fittings and carpet; the waves are the dark blue-green of a rather stormy sea.

Wooden pelmet
The deep wooden pelmet, made of tongued-and-grooved boards and painted to match the walls, lines up with the built-in cupboards and the edge of the bath. It gives the room a finished look and makes the bath seem much more private.

Round mirror
The white porthole-shaped mirror has a deep outline made of a delicate looking plastic which has a shell-like colour.

Shower screen
A fixed screen is an efficient choice and more in keeping than a shower curtain which could look fussy in this room.

Wood panelling
Tongued-and-grooved boards, fixed to a framework of battens, give the walls an interesting texture and have a nautical appeal.

The aquamarine colour suggests the sea in summer with sunlight filtering through.

Fixtures and flooring
The bathroom suite and the carpet are in closely related goldy-beige tones which bring to mind a warm sandy beach.

Lace curtain
The choice of a plain glass window, with its cream lace half-curtain and the view of foliage outside, prevents the room from becoming too austere.

A STREAMLINED BATHROOM

A windowless bathroom could be dark and rather oppressive. In this room the problem has been overcome by the careful choice of an almost all-white scheme so that fittings blend in with the walls, floor and ceiling. Because white gives maximum light reflection, the bathroom looks light and everything seems much bigger and more spacious than it actually is.

Small amounts of strong red in contrast to the white and clever use of mirrors and glass all help to add more interest to the room scheme.

Hairdryer
This modern wall-mounted hairdryer is conveniently placed for use. It fits in with the slightly futuristic look of the whole room.

Mirror trickery
There are two narrow strips of mirror: on the wall and at the bottom of the bath panel. These help make the room look longer and lighter and reflect maximum light.

White background
Colouring the whole shell of the room in light-reflecting white and choosing white sanitary fittings helps to make the room look light and spacious.

Glass shelves
Floor-to-ceiling open glass shelves house a supply of towels, flannels and toiletries. These shelves offer as much storage as a tall cupboard and blend well with the rest of the room.

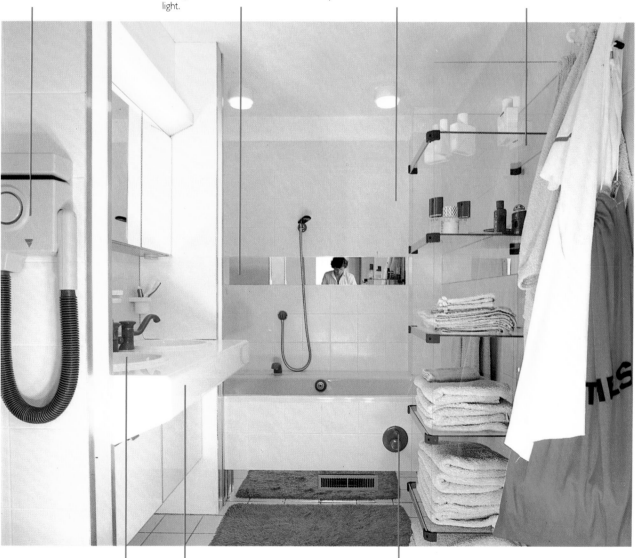

Wall-mounted basin
This hand basin is wall-mounted and cantilevered, which means the plumbing is hidden behind panelling. This gives you maximum floor space.

Modular bathroom furniture
This neat wall unit has been bought as a complete package to include double basins, mirrored wall cabinet, and overhead light. It packs maximum activities into minimum space.

Stark contrast
Splashes of red add dramatic interest to an otherwise monochromatic colour scheme. This only works well if the splashes of red are all the same shade like the laundry bag, bathmat, taps and fittings.

CREATING A GARDEN MOOD

A ground floor room and a glass-roofed lean-to have been knocked together to create a bathroom/dressing room with a look of luxury. The sloping glazed roof makes the room seem open and light and gives it a conservatory atmosphere. The room theme stems from this.

The colour scheme is green and white and a trellis pattern is repeated throughout the room on the walls and curtains to reflect the garden theme. Old-fashioned fixtures and fittings are more suited to the relaxed mood of this room than more modern ones.

Panels and border
Painting the wall panels and border green and covering them with white trellis gives a distinct impression of a pergola. To achieve this you could use garden trellis.

Climbing flowers
When these pretty flower-strewn patterned curtains are drawn the look of the garden is still retained in the bathroom.

Unfitted look
An old-fashioned roll-top bath, free-standing towel horse, brass taps and brass fittings make the bathroom look and feel cosy and 'lived-in'.

Reflections
Two large mirrors, framed by trellis, add to the feeling of space and light and appear to give glimpses of a whole suite of other garden rooms.

Washstand look
Marble top and brass taps give this vanity unit something of the look of a washstand, which works well with the old-style bath and accessories. With its roomy cupboard underneath it is also a practical choice. The basin is sunk below the worktop surface so there is no lip surround under which soap and dirt can collect. It is important, however, to make sure the basin is fitted and sealed properly.

Floor tiles
Unpolished terracotta floor tiles work well with the room's conservatory theme. Their old-fashioned look complements the Victorian bath and towel horse.

Painted bath
Painting the outside of the bath in a light terracotta colour with a matt, marble-effect finish is in perfect harmony with the earthy shades of the floor tiles.

BATHS AND BASINS

Buying a bathroom suite is an important step – it usually has to last a lifetime – so consider your options carefully.

BATH SIZES
The British Standard bath size is 1,700mm × 700mm wide and the average height is 500-610mm. Lower sides are usually better for small children, but the elderly often prefer higher sides to climb over – they don't have to bend over so far when getting in or out. Try a bath for size in the shop before buying it.

This chapter deals with baths and basins while the following chapters look at toilets, bidets, showers and accessories.

First and foremost the baths and basins in your house should reflect the washing habits and needs of your family. **Shape and size** are therefore important to get right; if members of your family are tall or you have children who bathe together, consider a larger-than-usual bath. If a basin is too shallow, when the taps are turned on, the water will just splash straight out. If you plan to wash clothes in your basin, make sure that is is deep and large enough for this. It should also be on a pedestal rather than wall hung, as this gives it extra strength to take the strain of pressing and wringing out washing in it.

Extras Check if the front and side panels are inclusive in the price of the bath. With the rectangular-shaped standard baths they are usually extra. Decide if you need to buy the panels. You may want to continue the floor covering in your bathroom up the side of the bath or even panel the bath with decorative tiles.

Taps are additional buys and can be quite pricey – especially the more modern ones. Check where the tap holes are in the bath or basin to make sure they suit the layout of your bathroom. Ask if you can choose where they are sited. And if you are going to fit a shower over the bath, check that the bath surface is non-slip.

Plumbing Consult a plumber early on in your plans or you could end up buying a cheap and cheerful bathroom suite only to have to spend much more money sorting out plumbing problems. Make sure the plumber is well established and try to find one who is a registered member of the Institute of Plumbers.

MATERIALS USED

Enamel on cast iron or steel Cast iron is the traditional base material for baths, but these days, steel is a cheaper and lighter alternative. The bath shape is moulded from iron or steel and it is either sprayed with or dipped in porcelain enamel or vitreous china and fired in a furnace. This gives the sanitaryware a smooth, and hygienic surface and results in a rigid and very hardwearing bath. It is, however, cold to the touch.

Use a non-abrasive bath cleaner and mild cream cleaner to clean. Treat with care, as enamel can chip off and can only be repaired by re-enamelling the whole bath.

Acrylic is easy to mould and so is ideal for making interesting and unusual shaped baths. (There are very few acrylic basins available.) The acrylic itself is reinforced with fibre glass to give it strength and mounted on to a galvanized steel frame. It makes light, easy-to-install baths, which are warm to the touch, but can be scratched. Check the thickness of the acrylic – if it is too thin, it tends to crack and split – the thickness is reflected in the price.

Clean with a liquid cleaner. Never use harsh abrasives. Remove stains with washing-up liquid or soap. Slight scratches can be smoothed out with liquid metal polish.

Fibre glass Baths made of fibre glass make up a small but luxury end of the market. They are built by hand in layers on a mould and, as only the top layer is coated with colour, any deep scratch shows up, revealing the base colour. They are warm, light and relatively easy to install. Only use liquid cleaners and avoid abrasives which can remove the surface colour.

Vitreous china is the main material used to make basins. It is a clay which is fired in a kiln at a very high temperature and then glazed to give it a tough and hygienic seal. It is hardwearing but care must be taken not to drop heavy objects in the basin as the china is liable to crack or chip. With age the glaze will gradually begin to craze (develop fine cracks). Clean with mild detergent and avoid abrasives.

BATH SHAPES

STANDARD RECTANGULAR
Style The British Standard size is 1700mm × 700mm, but there are larger and smaller versions on the market. If you are going to shower in the bath, the flatter the base is, the better.
In use These are usually fitted into a corner, but it is possible to fit them at right angles to a wall, allowing access to the bath from both sides.

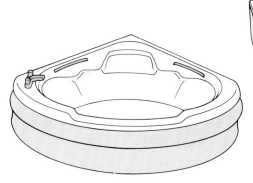

CORNER
Style These are usually made of acrylic because it moulds into shapes so easily. Allow a 1400mm × 1400mm space for a corner bath in your bathroom.
In use Look out for models with built-in shelf/seat ledges. Corner baths hold slightly more water than the average bath.

CONTOURED
Style Usually made in acrylic, these baths are shaped or waisted in the middle, tracing the outline of a human body.
In use They are very comfortable and are more economical on hot water than the standard shaped bath.

WHIRLPOOL

Style Also known as spa baths or Jacuzzis. Small nozzles set in sides of the bath pump out water under pressure into the bath when it is full. They are more expensive than ordinary baths.

In use Very relaxing especially after hard physical exercise, as the movement of the water massages the body.

TRADITIONAL

Style This old Victorian-shaped, free-standing bath is enjoying a revival. It usually stands on small ball and claw legs. Although original cast iron models are still available, reproduction glass fibre types are cheaper.

In use Look for reproduction Victorian-style freestanding taps to complement this bath.

SIT IN

Style This squat, square bath mimics the oriental soaking tub. It is ideal for the small bathroom and easily doubles up as a shower.

In use It has one or two built-in seats. Ideal for the elderly or disabled.

BASIN SHAPES

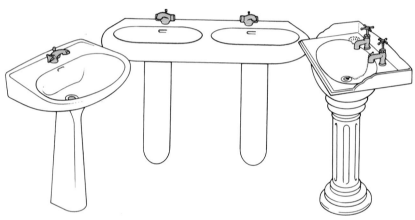

PEDESTAL

Style A pedestal basin is made up of two pieces – the bowl and pedestal. The pedestal is a supportive stem, which in turn hides the plumbing. It is available in many shapes and sizes, old and new styles. There are even double pedestals, supporting twin basins for a large or en suite bathroom.

In use Even when mounted on pedestals, basins still need fixing to the wall. One of their disadvantages is that, on average, they stand around 780-800mm high, so the height is fixed. This is too high for most young children. The pedestal does, however, take up floor space, which could in smaller bathrooms be put to much better use.

COLOUR

Many of the colours for baths and basins are British Standard colours, which means many different sanitaryware manufacturers produce identical colours, each coded with an identical number. This also applies to many tile manufacturers, so you should have no trouble in finding tiles to match your suite.

The same colour on a china basin can vary when reproduced on an acrylic bath. Remember that the colour of your suite will dictate your bathroom colour scheme – white is the most versatile as it tends to blend well with most other colours. Dark colours will show up stains, soap marks and hard water deposits.

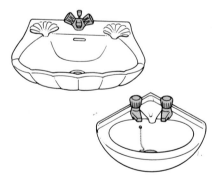

WALL MOUNTED

Style These basins vary from larger-than-standard size to tiny hand rinse units designed only for cloakrooms. They are hung from the wall so the pipework is usually exposed, although you can buy a half pedestal especially manufactured for wall-hung basins.

In use They are especially good where floor space is limited.

COUNTER TOP BASINS

Style These come in a variety of shapes to be sunken into counter tops, washstands or vanity units. They are also available as basin and counter top, moulded as one piece in ceramic, acrylic or marble-effect plastic.

In use Cupboards or vanity units into which these basins are set hide plumbing and provide extra bathroom storage space.

UNUSUAL SHAPES

Style Basins come in many different shapes and sizes. A triangular-shaped basin fits neatly into the corner of your bathroom so is practical and space saving. Other shapes can simply be installed for decorative purposes.

In use For unusual-shaped basins, especially corner-shaped basins, there is often no room for the taps, so consider mounting taps on wall above.

BATHROOM TAPS, WCs AND BIDETS

The style and shape of sanitaryware and the type of taps that you choose, set the whole mood of your bathroom.

Although the modern bathroom is often one of the smaller rooms in a house, it is one of the most frequently used. Space should be handled carefully as there are a definite number of essential bathroom fitments; the water closet or WC is one of them. The bidet, so popular on the continent, is becoming more common in Britain and is usually included in ranges of suites.

Bathroom taps are additional buys. The range on the market is growing and becoming more sophisticated.

TAPS

If you are renewing taps, your choice is restricted by the size and number of tapholes already in your bath, basin or bidet. But if you are starting from scratch, you can choose from taps of all different shapes and styles.

There are a variety of finishes available; from the conventional chromium-plated to stainless steel, brass and gold, as well as coloured plastic taps.

Look out for taps which conform to the British Standard BS5412/3 Part 1 and 2. It guarantees that the tap allows water to pass through at an acceptable and practical rate. All taps should satisfy your local water authority's by-laws, which safeguard against water wastage or contamination. For more information refer to the Directory of Fittings and Materials at your local library.

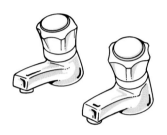

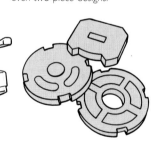

PILLAR TAPS
Style This is the conventional style tap, usually bought in a pair – one for the cold water, the other for the hot. The water supply pipe to the pillar tap usually comes from below, so the tap must be mounted on a horizontal surface such as a bath or basin rim.

In use The modern pillar taps are usually much smaller and neater than the traditional types.

MIXER TAPS
Style This mixes the hot and cold water supply into one central tap. There are basically two mixer types: the dual flow mixer tap appears to mix both hot and cold water through a central tap/spout, but in fact each supply runs along its own separate channel in the tap/spout.

A 'true' mixer really does mix hot and cold together, but it must be installed by a plumber, so both water

supplies are of equal pressure.

In use A mixer tap, which has to be plumbed into the bath, basin or bidet, though just one taphole, is known as a monobloc mixer, (above left). A three-piece mixer, (above), can only be fitted to fittings with three tapholes; one for the tap and two holes for the controls. Both the dual flow and 'true' mixer come as either monoblocs, three-piece or even two-piece designs.

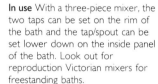

BATH MIXER
Style Bath mixers also come as monoblocs and two- or three-piece types. Many come with shower hose and a diverter lever to channel the water from the tap through the hose and out of the shower head.

In use With a three-piece mixer, the two taps can be set on the rim of the bath and the tap/spout can be set lower down on the inside panel of the bath. Look out for reproduction Victorian mixers for freestanding baths.

SINGLE LEVER TAP
Style On this type of tap a lever controls the flow of water. Usually the more the lever is raised, the greater the flow of water. Most types are in fact mixer taps, so the lever moves to the left or right to

give hot or cold water.

In use Washers are replaced by discs, usually ceramic ones (shown enlarged, above). These are durable and resistant to limescale. They form a water-tight seal in the tap, so dripping shouldn't be a problem.

BIDET MIXER
Style The most basic mixer tap for the bidet just mixes hot and cold water. Look out for taps with spouts that swivel to allow more room for washing. Some bidet mixers offer

additional adjustable nozzles, to give a directional spray (douche).

In use If fitting a sophisticated mixer, check with your water authority or plumber that it conforms to regulations.

WASTES
Basin and bath water is let out through a waste (or plug hole). The conventional waste is plugged with a plastic or rubber plug hanging on a chain from the overflow outlet.

The more modern pop-up waste does away with a plug on a chain. When a lever (usually part of the tap) is pressed or alternatively when a knob (set in the bath panel) is turned, a lid or cover over the waste automatically pops up to let out the water.

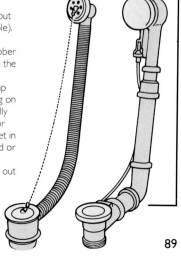

WCs

A water closet or WC is usually made of vitreous china, because it is non-porous and therefore hygienic. WCs consist of a pan containing water and cistern which holds the water for flushing away waste.

The flush is operated by a handle or similar device. Some cisterns come with a dual flush offering a choice of a full or half flush to use as necessary.

Wash-down This is the most common flushing mechanism. It uses a large flow of water which scours the whole inner surface of the pan and is powerful enough to discharge the contents of the pan. It is efficient but can be rather noisy.

Syphonic This is an alternative flushing method. It operates by syphoning (drawing out) the water. It is quiet and efficient.

Shredding and pumping unit This is a device which can be fitted to a WC to shred and pump the discharge electronically. It relays waste through a much narrower pipe (small bore), so the WC can be installed almost anywhere in the house because the narrower pipe is easily run behind walls. You can also buy a WC fitted with the unit.

Traps Like all other bathroom fittings, the WC pan has a trap (a bend in the outpipe), which holds water to form a seal, stopping drain smells from coming into the house. As the trap is an integral part of the outlet pipe on your WC, check which sort you need.

If the outlet pipe disappears straight into the wall behind the WC, buy a horizontal or P-trap WC, if it disappears into the floor below, buy an S-trap WC.

Cistern, soil pipes and plumbing can be hidden behind a false wall or panel – this is known as ducted installation.

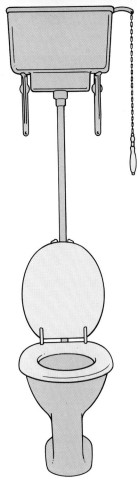

CLOSE COUPLED

Style A close-coupled WC incorporates cistern and pan in a single construction.

In use This saves space and gives a very neat appearance.

BACK TO THE WALL

Style The outlet connections (soil pipe, for example) are completely contained in the ceramic shape of the WC.

In use The overall appearance is neat and its compact shape is easy to clean round.

WALL HUNG

Style This WC is mounted on an invisible bracket that runs below the floor and behind the wall.

In use This leaves the floor area around the WC completely clear. It should be complemented by a ducted (boxed off) cistern.

HIGH-LEVEL

Style This is the traditional arrangement – the cistern is set high on the wall above the pan. They are joined by a length of flush pipe.

In use This has been almost totally updated by the low-level cistern – the cistern sits just above the pan, joined by a shorter pipe called the flushbend.

BIDETS

The bidet is a low-level wash basin for personal hygiene. It is also just the right height for children to wash in and, in Britain, it is often used as a foot bath.

Most bidets are made from vitreous china to match the shapes and colours of the basin and WC.

Over-the-rim A bidet is supplied by both hot and cold running water and the basic type is filled over-the-rim in the same way as a basin is filled.

Below-the-rim The more sophisticated and expensive models are filled by a method called below-the-rim, which means that the bidet is warmer to sit on than the over-the-rim type, as a stream of hot water is sent round the rim before the bowl is filled, some also have a douche spray option.

Before buying, check with your water authority that it conforms to regulations, as below-the-rim models are banned by some authorities.

WALL HUNG

Style All the pipework for the bidet is ducted (concealed behind a panel or false wall).

In use A wall-hung bidet is usually chosen to match a wall-hung WC.

FLOOR STANDING

Style The pipework can be visible, like a low level WC or concealed like the back-to-the-wall WC.

In use This should be set at the same height as the WC.

SIZES AND POSITIONING

Space shortage is a common problem in a bathroom and the positioning of WCs and bidets is often restricted because of plumbing requirements.

WCs The size of a WC varies from one manufacturer to another. But as a guideline the pan should be at a height to be comfortable to sit on. Allow for a floor space of about 140cm× 70cm wide for a WC with a cistern. This gives you enough space not to feel cramped using it. The pan must be covered with a wooden or plastic seat. If buying plastic, look for tough, rigid plastic, which gives more support to the thighs, and is less likely to crack.

On the modern low-level WC the cistern is usually about 75-100cm high. The high-level cistern is more like 180cm high.

A low-level WC takes up more room than a high-level, because the cistern sits closely above the pan so the pan is further forward than if the cistern is 180cm above it.

Less space can be taken up with a low-level WC if you buy a new slim-line cistern.

Bidets A bidet is usually the same height as the WC – about 40cm. It should be sited as close to the WC as possible.

WATER SUPPLIES

Regulations for the plumbing installations of bidets vary from water board to water board. Your plumber should advise you on local requirements, but generally the over-the-rim type is quite straight forward to install, while the below-the-rim type needs special installation to stop what is known as back syphonage, which can cause water contamination.

This type of bidet must have its own cold water supply pipe running directly from the cold water cistern and no other pipes or fittings should be connected to this pipe.

The hot water supply must run from the highest pipe taken off the hot water cylinder and again no other pipes or fittings should be connected to it. Some bidet plumbing systems require that waste water is discharged via the soil pipe.

CHOOSING A SHOWER

Showering has many advantages – perhaps the most important is that it's a quick, easy and economical way to wash.

A shower uses one-fifth of the water used to run a bath, which not only saves on water, but also on heating bills. It is also quicker to shower than to bath and, if you choose to install a shower instead of a bath, it takes up much less floor space. Many people consider a shower is more hygienic than soaking in a bath, as soap and grime are constantly being rinsed away in the shower by clean, running water. Follow our guidelines on how to choose the best shower for your home.

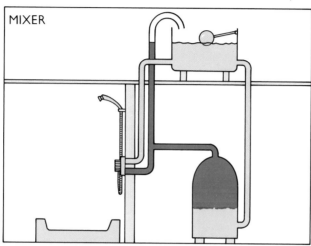

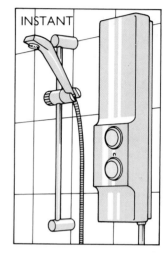

TYPES OF SHOWER
MIXER SHOWER
Style This kind of shower (right), takes its cold water from the storage cistern and mixes it with hot water from the hot water cylinder.
In use The bottom of the cold water cistern should be at least 1m higher than the actual shower head. (This distance is called the head of water.) This ensures there is enough pressure to create a reasonable spray of water. A bigger head or difference between these two gives a more powerful spray.

Moving the cistern higher is often a simple job, if this isn't possible, fit a booster pump to compensate.
Watchpoint The biggest problem is what is known as a draw-off – this can happen when a tap is turned on or a WC flushed, while the shower is running, cutting down the flow to the shower (which can make the shower uncomfortably hot). Avoid this by giving the shower its own cold water supply direct from the cold storage tank, so that it does not take cold water from a supply pipe supplying other fittings.

POSITIONING YOUR SHOWER

Over the bath Any type of shower can be installed over a bath. It is the obvious location as the drainage for the shower water is already there. As you have to stand in the bath, the base should be as flat and wide as possible and preferably have a non-slip finish. Otherwise, buy a non-slip shower mat or wooden slatted platform to stand on.

Showering in the bath usually gives you more space to stand away from the shower spray, so it is possible to shower without, for example, getting your hair wet.
Corner or alcove showers If you don't want a shower over the bath, then a corner or alcove shower is another choice. This means you can have your shower in a room other than the bathroom.

With a corner shower, the two adjacent walls, which form the inside of the shower, need to be totally waterproof. Tiled walls are ideal, as long as the grout used in between the tiles is waterproof. With alcove showers, all three of the walls need to be waterproof.
Freestanding units These can be made of plastic, strengthened safety glass or coated steel. They come with four panels, shower tray,

BATH MIXER SHOWER
Style This is the most basic and cheapest type of shower, taking its two water supplies direct from the bath taps via a mixer tap which has a shower diverter.
In use The same rules about the minimum head of water which apply to a mixer shower, also apply to this type.

INSTANT SHOWER
Style This usually takes its water from the rising cold water mains. The water is heated to a set temperature by an electric or gas heater in a splash-proof, wall-mounted case to give instant hot water for the shower.
In use Electric versions are the most

common (above right). The only drawback is that when the temperature is adjusted it alters the rate of water through the heater, so the choice is less water at a higher temperature or more at a lower temperature.
Watchpoint Built-in thermostats automatically keep water at required temperature.

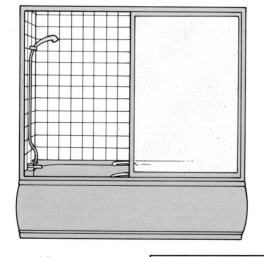

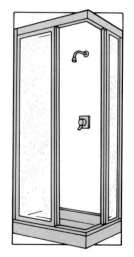

plumbing and fittings, so you don't have to rely on any of the interior walls as frames. Some have tops, too, to stop vapour escaping and causing condensation in the room. Kit forms are often the cheapest way to buy them.

Some are dual purpose – ideal for the bedroom or studio flat (where space is limited) – and double up as vanity units and washbasins. They also have stow-away shower trays and fittings for when the shower is not being used.

SHOWER TRAYS
A shower tray is the base which you stand in if you have a corner/alcove or separate shower unit.

It can be made from vitreous china, glazed fireclay (a tougher form of china), acrylic or vitreous enamelled steel, in colours to match bathroom suites.

On average, a tray measures between 700mm and 900mm square, although bigger or smaller sizes in different shapes, including triangular ones for corner showers, are available.

If you plan to tile the walls around the shower tray, look for one with a special tiling lip. If the shower is to replace a bath, consider a shower tray with a foot area and moulded-in seat so you can shower sitting down.

ENCLOSURES

Shower curtains These are an easy-to-fit and relatively cheap shower enclosure. They are waterproof, washable or can be wiped down and are usually made from PVC, nylon, or coated cotton. Many are treated so they won't become mouldy.

However, you can hang a shower curtain made of any fabric if you line the side which receives most of the splashing with a plastic curtain. Look for non-rusting hooks and eyelets.

Curtains hang from rails or poles made of a light, rust-proof material such as aluminium or plastic. They can be fastened to the wall with screws and brackets or come spring-loaded so the pole lodges itself firmly in-between two walls. Curtains can form either one, two, or three sides of an over-the-bath or corner/alcove shower.

Bath screens are used with over-the-bath showers as alternatives to wet curtains. They are usually made of glass or toughened plastic. The screen is fixed to the side of the bath to stop the shower water splashing over the edge. Some screens run along half the length of the bath. They can be fixed rigid or hinged, so they can be swivelled to allow the user to get in easier. Others are made up in two or three separate pieces, each hinged together to fold like a concertina.

Another variety is the sliding screen; two screens run along the entire length of the bath and slide backwards and forwards.

Shower screens and doors Screens for shower cubicles, like those for the bath, are usually made from toughened glass or plastic. Shower doors are usually the same as screens but they hinge, pivot, slide or fold open and shut.

SHOWER HEADS

The shower head, (also known as a handset if it can be detached from the wall and hand held), should be fixed above the height of the user, or alternatively at shoulder level.

Magnetic head A magnetic shower head supplied with water via a flexible hose, can be positioned anywhere on the walls of a steel shower unit.

Clip-on head This shower head with a flexible hose is fastened by a clip to the shower wall so it can be detached.

Head on slide rail Most instant showers have the shower head on a slide rail. The angle of the spray can be adjusted, so can the height, by sliding the handset up and down the rail. The head is on a flexible pipe so it can be hand held.

Brush head There is a shower head on the market which is like a brush. It can be detached and used for washing while still spraying water.

Fixed head This means the height of the shower is permanently fixed, although the head can be swivelled to alter the angle of the spray. It is plumbed to a specific height and the pipework to the head is usually ducted (run behind panels or tiling). There are many different styles, but the more traditional type has the supply pipe showing.

Body spray and jets Some luxury freestanding shower units not only spray water at the user via a shower head, but also via a series of pipes.

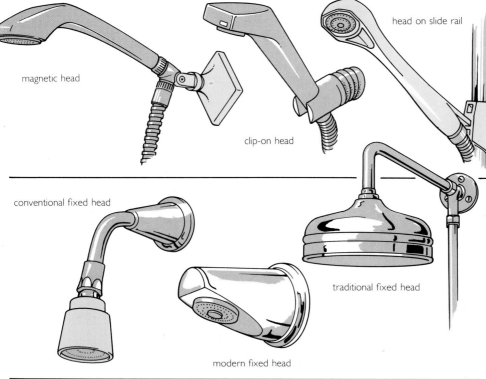

magnetic head

clip-on head

head on slide rail

brush head

conventional fixed head

modern fixed head

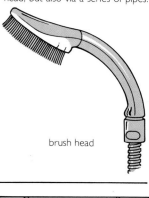

traditional fixed head

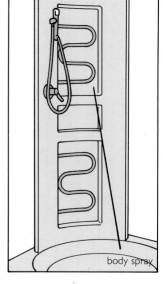

body spray

PLUMBING AND INSTALLATION

Many showers only operate if there is sufficient water pressure. Your plumber should be able to advise you on this, and your local water authority should be able to tell you the pressure of your incoming mains water. If pressures in your house are very low or very high, check what pressures the shower operates on before making a purchase.

Instant gas showers must be installed by a qualified gas fitter and instant electric showers by a qualified electrician. (Water and electricity can be a lethal combination so make sure before making a purchase that the shower has been designed and tested to the British Standard 3456.) Most waste pipes from separate shower trays should be reasonably close to the soil pipe, so consult a plumber.

SHOWER SAFETY

Water and soap make a slippery combination, so a grab rail in the wall of the shower area is useful – especially for the elderly.

Sliding shower doors or those hinged to open inwards prevent drips on the floor in front of the shower – so should cut down the risk of slipping.

A soap dish recessed into the wall is also a sensible feature. Look out for a soap dish which clips onto the shower head slide rail (right); so it can be raised or lowered to suit the user. Alternatively buy soap on a rope or a container of liquid soap that can be hung up.

A shower seat is especially useful for the elderly or disabled to sit on while taking a shower. It does not have to be built into the shower wall, but can be bought as a ready-made fitting (far right). The plastic slatted seat folds up flush against the wall when not in use.

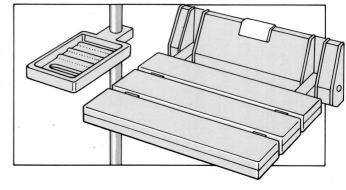

BATHROOM ACCESSORIES

A bathroom wouldn't function properly without the simple accessories that make bath times so much easier.

As well as being attractive, bathroom accessories should be practical additions to your bathroom, for keeping a whole host of bits and pieces tidy and easily accessible.

Most items can be selected from large ranges and are usually made from easy-clean materials – choose from plastic, glass, china, wood, brass, stainless steel and chrome. Some accessories even come with gold plating. There are prices to suit everyone, from a few pounds to thousands of pounds.

The biggest choice of accessories comes in the wall-mounted ranges. You'll find toilet roll holders, toothbrush holders, flannel and robe hooks, towel rails and rings, shelves, soap dishes and wall cabinets. In addition, there are freestanding accessories such as toilet brushes, waste bins and towel racks.

STORAGE ACCESSORIES

Toiletries, spare toilet rolls, medicines and cleaning equipment can either be displayed on wall-mounted shelving or stored away inside a cupboard. A good sized bathroom cabinet with a mirror on the front is invaluable – especially if it has an integral light and a shaver point.

Cheaper models are moulded plastic bath bars made especially to hang on the wall above the bath or basin. Most have shelves, but some also incorporate useful additions such as toothbrush holders and a cupboard.

TOILET ACCESSORIES

Give your toilet a new look by swopping the old seat for a new one, or top it with a fluffy fabric cover. Most covers come as a set with a shaped pedestal mat, and optional bath mat.

MATERIALS

Plastic accessories come in a range of pastel, primary and neutral shades to co-ordinate with the most popular sanitaryware colours.

Wood accessories tend to come in just two shades: pine to match light, country style rooms, and dark mahogany which is often teamed with china and brass for a traditional feel.

Metal Cheapest of all is chrome but you can choose from bronze, brass and stainless steel (as well as gold plate).

Ceramic If made by a sanitaryware manufacturer, ceramic accessories should match your suite exactly. If you are planning to tile your walls, there are some pretty ceramic accessories which are made to insert into a standard tile space; others are simply surface-mounted.

TYPES OF ACCESSORIES

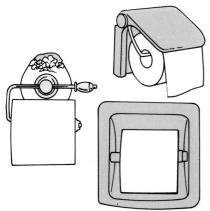

TOILET ROLL HOLDER
Style A metal, plastic or wooden dowel that slips through the centre of the toilet roll. Some are recessed into the wall and others come with musical chimes!
In use Check that the holder allows the toilet roll to run freely – some designs need two hands to use them.

TOWEL RAIL
Style Can be wall-mounted, freestanding or attached to a radiator. They come in plastic, wood or a range of different metals. Heated versions are also available.
In use It's a good idea to place the rail over a radiator so that wet towels can dry while they are hanging – cheaper than a heated rail.

TOWEL RING
Style A round or semi-circular ring made of wood, metal or plastic which is always wall-mounted.
In use Ideal to use where space is limited. Place close to the basin or on a door.
Watchpoint Towels which are not hung flat tend to dry more slowly.

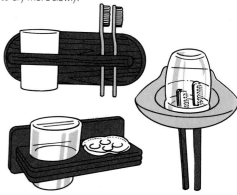

TOOTHBRUSH HOLDER
Style A small slotted rack to hold toothbrushes. Many holders incorporate a space for a glass or mug and a tube of toothpaste.
In use A handy way of keeping toothbrushes clean and ready to use.

ROBE HOOK
Style Small hook, usually made of wood, metal or plastic, attached to the wall on a bracket.
In use For hanging dressing gowns or robes while in the bathroom.

FLANNEL RACK
Style A small bank of hooks or knobs.
In use Position the rack over the basin or bath to catch drips from wet flannels – over the radiator is a viable alternative.

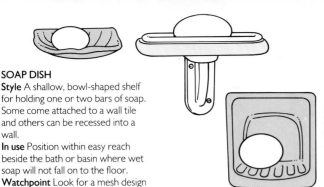
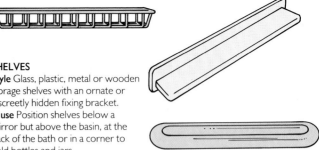

SOAP DISH
Style A shallow, bowl-shaped shelf for holding one or two bars of soap. Some come attached to a wall tile and others can be recessed into a wall.
In use Position within easy reach beside the bath or basin where wet soap will not fall on to the floor.
Watchpoint Look for a mesh design or one with a ridged base that will stop the soap from becoming soft.

CABINETS
Style Moulded from plastic or wood-framed, most cabinets have one or more interior shelves. Some have mirrored doors, built-in lights and a shaving socket. Corner models are available.
In use Position the cabinet where it won't be in the way – in a corner or above the basin are practical.
Watchpoint When storing medicines or cleaning products, choose a cabinet with a childproof lock.

SHELVES
Style Glass, plastic, metal or wooden storage shelves with an ornate or discreetly hidden fixing bracket.
In use Position shelves below a mirror but above the basin, at the back of the bath or in a corner to hold bottles and jars.

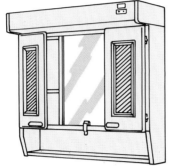

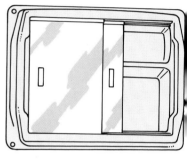

SHOWER CADDIES
Style Made in a wire mesh or from plastic with drainage holes, these cabinets are designed for use in a shower since water can drain straight through them.
In use For holding soap, shampoo and flannels while using the shower. Position so that you can easily reach it when showering: next to the shower unit is preferable to below it so that water doesn't soften the soap.

BATH SHELVES/CUPBOARDS
Style Moulded in one piece from plastic, these rigid storage holders are made in colours to match sanitaryware and to fit alongside standard size baths.
In use Tall units can be fitted at the end of a bath or over a basin with space to hold toothbrushes and soap, as well as a shelf and a mirror. Long, thin versions are made to fit along the length of your bath to hold toiletries.

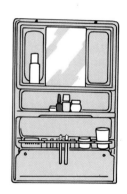

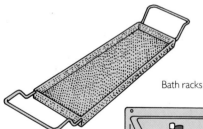

Bath racks

Bath bar

BATH RACK
Style Usually made of metal, often plastic-coated, the rack sits across the width of the bath and is used to hold bath sponges and toiletries.
In use Make sure your rack has holes punched in the base to allow water to drain away freely and stop the soap becoming soggy.

BATH BAR
Style Long plastic unit designed to hang on the wall alongside the bath. For holding accessories such as toiletries, nail brushes and sponges. Many designs also incorporate a small mirror.
In use Position on the wall next to the bath. Directly above is the most suitable place.
Watchpoint Not intended for freestanding baths.

TOILET BRUSH
Style A pot or stand with a detachable brush that is used for cleaning the loo.
In use Some pots can be filled with disinfectant so that the brush can be sterilised when it is not in use. As toilet brushes are usually placed next to the toilet, it is a good idea to choose a co-ordinating style and colour.

TOILET SEAT
Style Many different styles of toilet seats are available in plastic, ceramic or wood. There is a huge range of colours and finishes to select from.
In use Each seat comes complete with fixings so it's an easy job to remove the old one and fit the new.
Watchpoint Not all seats fit all WCs, so measure up carefully or be sure to take a paper template with you when choosing a replacement.

SLIP MAT
Style A square, oblong or oval rubber mat with suction pads on the underside to hold it firmly in place on the bath or shower tray surface.
In use Lay a mat in a bath or shower tray to produce a safe and completely non-slip surface – especially useful for the very young or the elderly.
Watchpoint In a shower, make sure the mat doesn't cover the waste hole of the shower tray.

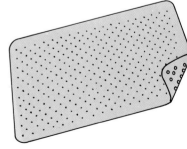

INDEX

PHOTOGRAPHIC CREDITS
Front cover MFI, 1 BC Sanitan, 2-3 EWA/Rodney Hyett, 4-5 Boots Bathrooms, 6 Crown Paints, 9 Bosch, 10(t) David Hicks, 10(b) Marbodal of Sweden, 11(t) Laconite, 11(b) Caprez, 12(t) Syndication International, 12(b) Fanfare 2000 by Fordham, 13(t) EWA/Clive Helm, 13(b) National Magazine Co/Dennnis Stone, 14 Poggenpohl, 15 National Magazine Co/William Douglas, 16,18(t) Ideal Standard, 18(b) Syndication International, 19 Mantaleda, 20(t) Cover Plus from Woolworth, 20(bl) EWA/Spike Powell, 20(br) Jerry Tubby/Eaglemoss, 21(t) EWA/Julian Nieman, 21(b) EWA/Clive Helm, 22 Syndication International, 24-5 EWA, 24(b) Syndication International, 25(t) Bill McLaughlin, 26 Jalag, 28(t) EWA/Neil Lorimer, 28(b) CP Hart, 29 Arcaid/Richard Bryant, 30 Cristal Tiles, 31 EWA/Andreas von Einsiedel, 32(t) Ron Sutherland, 32(b) Arcaid/Lucinda Lambton, 33 H & R Johnson, 34 Cover Plus from Woolworth, 35 EWA/Michael Nicholson, 36 Dulux Paints, 37(t) PWA International, 37(b) EWA/Clive Helm, 38(t) Ken Kirkwood, 38(b) Grub Street, 39 Pipe Dreams, 40-41 B&Q DIY Centres, 40(t) Twyfords, 41 Pipe Dreams, 42(t) Star Interiors, 42(b) Cover Plus from Woolworth, 43 Bosch, 44(t) EWA, 44(b) Svedberg, 45(t) Spectrum Shelving, 45(b) CP Hart, 46 Berglen Tapmate, 47 Bo Appeltoft, 48-9(t) Wickes Building Supplies Ltd, 48(b) Sommer Allibert, 50 Smallbone, 51(t) Fordham, 51(b) EWA, 52(tl) National Magazine Co/Dennis Stone, 52(tr) Syndication International, 52(b) Vymura, 53 Aquarius Bathrooms, 54(t) Stelrad, 54(b) Pipe Dreams, 55(t) Pinelog Products, 55(bl) Zess, 55(br) Aqua Dial, 56-7 Twyfords, 56(b) Twyfords, 57(tr) Jalag, 57(b) John Suett/Eaglemoss, 58(t) Fitness in Home, 58(b) Harrod of Lowestoft, 59 Tilemart, 60(t) Cover Plus from Woolworth, 60(b) Next Interior, 61(t) Richard Paul, 62(t) B J Arnull, 62(b) The Original Bathroom Company, 63(t) Cristal Tiles, 63(b) CP Hart, 64(t) Allia, 64(c,b) B J Arnull, 65 Syndication International, 69 Jalag/Ingo Kirschnik, 70 Syndication International, 72-3(b) Leisure, 72(b) Matki, 73(b) Jalag, 74(t) EWA/Spike Powell, 74(b) EWA/Rodney Hyett, 75(b) EWA/Michael Dunne, 76 Twyfords, 77 Jalag/Peter Adams, 78 Twyfords, 79 Syndication International, 80(t) EWA/Rodney Hyett, 80(b) EWA/Spike Powell, 81 Camera Press, 82 National Magazine Co/Lucinda Lambton, 83 PWA International, 84 B&Q DIY Centres, 85 EWA, 86 EWA/Michael Dunne